Games of Persuasion

Exercises in Media Literacy

Dominic W. Moreo

Writers Club Press
San Jose New York Lincoln Shanghai

Games of Persuasion
Exercises in Media Literacy

Published by Writers Club Press
an imprint of iUniverse.com, Inc.

For information address:
iUniverse.com, Inc.
620 North 48th Street
Suite 201
Lincoln, NE 68504-3467
www.iuniverse.com

ISBN: 0-595-00321-4

Printed in the United States of America

For Bev

Epigraph

...*chance* favors the prepared mind.

—Louis Pasteur

It is not calumny or treachery that do the largest sum of mischief in the world. But it is the glistening and soft spoken lie; the amiable fallacy; the patriotic lie of the historian; the provident lie of the politician; the zealous lie of the partisan; the merciful lie of the friend, and the careless lie of each man to himself, that cast the black mystery over humanity...

—John Ruskin

Contents

Preface

Conversation is a game of circles.
—Ralph Waldo Emerson

Like rain, the messages of persuasion fall everywhere. And now a message from our "sponsor." Breathes a living person in America, from toddler to grandparent, who has not heard the familiar lead-in to still another "message" asking us to buy, to vote for, to stop this behavior, or to donate to this or that worthy cause? While commercials on TV shrink to twenty and ten seconds, their numbers multiply. Despite their volume and velocity, what are the ingredients of these messages? Do they always work? What are the limits of persuasion?

To answer these questions what follows is a primer on the craft, tricks, and techniques of persuasion. There are many public "players" of persuasion including advertisers, politicians, public relations firms, lobbyists, apostles of single issues, and, of course, the media holding a putative mirror to "reality." Whatever their motives and goals, the various players are practitioners by design, by happenstance and by inadvertence of persuasion in the public realm.

Thomas Babington Macaulay, the English historian noted, "The object of oratory alone is not truth, but persuasion." For the most part, conversation and persuasion play within a game of circles.

To obtain some leverage on this circular game, the first two chapters in linear fashion present a catalog of various devices that the practitioners of persuasion practice. How modern advertisers court the consumer is the subject of the following chapter. How politicians court the good citizen in roundabout manner with the aid of professional advertisers, public relations firms and other media consultants is examined in chapter four.

The following chapter explores the uses and abuses of street protests, demonstrations and violence. As an illustration of this type of "persuasion," the 1999 World Trade Organization's meeting in Seattle comes to mind.

Both chapters six and seven are concerned with the persuasive impact of condensed messages whether they are single frame political cartoonists or aphorists reducing behavior to a pithy generalization. Both the drawings and aphorisms are the bon-bons of thought, those mental insights and fireworks that bring at times chagrin and upon other occasion's nods of agreement and smiles.

To concentrate their effectiveness, citizens, consumers, businesses, trade unions and countless organizations resort to lobbying for their plank or cause. Lobbyists are not unlike cartoonists in focusing on a single aspect or issue to the detriment of all other matters. Unlike the messages directed at consumers and citizens, these slick agents of persuasion engage in building a critical mass of persuasion. Doing good would seem thus to be the antithesis of lobbying for a narrowly focused objective. However, chapter eight probes the persuasive powers of lobbyists and others who practice the arts of the "full-court-press."

Thomas Jefferson observed that a society might do without a government but no civil society could long endure without a free press. Is the press merely a communal megaphone or increasingly an instrument of persuasion? The final chapter explores these and related questions.

Finally a caveat is in order. Persuasion involving flattery and other forms of seduction in private affairs are beyond the scope of this work.

1

The Persuasion Game

To be, or not to be: that is the question:
—Shakespeare, *Hamlet*, Act III

In the "Republic of Entertainment", as Neal Gabler has written, to persuade one must tell a story. Better still turn the story into one's life movie! So powerful has the grip of entertainment on our psyche become that it has led to "the triumph of the senses over the mind, of emotion over reason, of chaos over order...of Dionysian abandon over Apollonian harmony." The prime example is of course MTV. It uses entertainment to sell entertainment; it uses stories to sell stories, with music as the tag line.

Does this mean that we can sit back and enjoy the ride whatever buttons the wizards behind the screen are pushing? Only if media illiteracy is welcomed. If not, to the traditional 3Rs we must add media literacy as a necessity in this age of information explosion and the Internet. What follows is an attempt to probe the images, messages and massages from the media.

Are persuasion and propaganda the same? The dictionary informs us that the latter is the use of various means of persuasion. A circular definition, indeed. Propaganda seeks to make someone believe something; or to cause someone to take action as a result of arguments, reasons, cajolery or coercion; or to win over someone by varied means from flattery to inducement.

During the First World War, propaganda was utilized by both sides using film, posters, press releases and rumors to paint the other side as inhuman, barbaric as, for example, the rumor that German troops bayoneted Belgian babies. Disinformation, even though the term was not used till the Cold War in the 1950s, was an important element in the propaganda arsenal. When the United States entered the First World War, the federal government established a Committee on Public Information headed by George Creel, which set out to emulate English and German agencies in this black and white warfare of words, images and misinformation.

By the 1930s in the land of Adolph Hitler's Third Reich, Dr. Josef Goebbels became its minister of propaganda. Propaganda in his hands meant the power to manipulate public opinion by sundry means of radio broadcasts, street-corner loudspeakers, and the press to spread deceit, lies and bigger lies. Repetition of messages became the norm. Today the term propaganda like Nazi Germany has fallen into disfavor and disuse. Yet propaganda is but one form, albeit at times crude, of persuasion.

Some would argue that a fundamental distinction between persuasion and education, properly understood, is that the former offers quick answers, shortcuts to thought, and mind massages while education raises questions, sees distinctions, and stoically notes that not all human and social problems have answers. The former, for example, is a welcome to a public meeting closed to non-believers while the latter involves a journey much like Diogenes searching for truth as well as good and wise people.

Propaganda and persuasion also can slip under the radar screen of the mind by posing as something else as when messages are disguised as "news" or "facts" or "research." An example that comes to mind is those late night television "infomercials" masquerading as straight news. Or when ads appear in the guise of newscasts.

Rather than as a black art, Jacques Ellul on the other hand sees the role of propaganda as an institutional necessity in a technological society to such an extent that propaganda and education are not antithetical discourses but complementary and symbiotic modes. For Ellul the effectiveness of propaganda depends to a large degree on its base of veracity. Typically many people equate propaganda with the dissemination solely of lies. But Ellul disagrees. In this context, for Ellul, propaganda may not only divide a population but also serve as an integrating mechanism. He states "Propaganda is called upon to solve problems created by technology, to play on maladjustments, and to integrate the individual into a technological world." For example, advertising seeks to integrate the consumer with the output of a modern economy, as we shall explore in chapter three.

Historically the term propaganda came into use for another purpose. Originally the term stemmed from the Catholic Church's establishment in 1633 of the *Congregation of the Propaganda* to preach and spread the doctrines of the church overseas. Thus as a set of instruments, propaganda may be used to satisfy in human beings both temporal and spiritual hungers. But for the Catholic Church it was also an institutional counter-attack to the challenge of the Reformation inaugurated in 1517 by Martin Luther.

Long ago Aristotle observed that man is a social animal. From that day forward, persuasion has been an indispensable part of social life. What follows is an attempt to provide a firm foot-hold from the daily overflow of messages bombarding us to buy and sell; to stop forest fires, litter, AIDS; or to vote for a candidate or cause; or to donate money and time to a worthy cause; or to donate blood. If we understand the tricks and the craft of persuasion, then we may if we wish resist the siren call of persuasion—or join the bandwagon. Not unlike a visit to Universal City where make-believe and shadows become reality, if we wish.

So what are the rules of the game of persuasion? Without further ado, welcome to the carnival of tricks and illusion, a veritable house of mirrors. To change metaphors, the siren calls of advertisers, along with the various scams of hucksters, and the pitches of politicians are as seductive and sweet as when Ulysses first heard the siren songs of temptation. No matter where we turn, the messages pour in relentlessly. Marshall McLuhan has asserted that the message and media are one. However we shall move on the opposite assumption that means and ends, message and context, degree and kind are not only worth delineating but vital to understanding and media literacy.

To begin with, this primer's format lends itself to understanding and immediate application. In the catalog of techniques that follows, we shall use trick to mean crafty procedure or practice; and concept to denote an abstract or general idea.

>>Trick 1: Card stacking—is the device whereby by omission and selective use of data in various genres of speeches, commercials, articles, books, letters, photos, motion pictures and television leads to a predetermined goal or outcome.
>>Examples:

1 "I like communists *like a hole in the head*."
2 "I like communists."
3 A photo of two men and *two women*.
4 The photo cropped by removing the two women.
5 A "balanced" report showing one group at prayer in church, while a second group is screaming obscenities on the street.

>>Comment: The first example involves politicians and other lobbying groups that use the collateral technique of "quoting" out of context their opponent's views, or by handing out documents, letters or photos that have been cropped by scissors and/or re-photographed or

rearranged. Today thanks to digitized computer manipulation even children can engage in this trick. The purpose of this "doctoring" is to produce unpleasant associations such as guilt by innuendo and guilt by association. If one of the two men is a pariah then the other suffers by proximity, which is the intent. The last example is a favorite of television news in that by selection and by order, you have card stacking in one seamless operation. And all so professional!

Another version of this tactic is to have the "favorite" politician looking composed and presidential while the opponent has his mouth open, his suit rumpled, and his hair tousled. In chapter nine, we shall explore the omissions and distortions of the press and television news.

Of all the techniques that follow whether tricks or concepts, the paramount one remains card stacking. The term comes naturally from card playing. In a reputable gambling casino, one expects that the house will use a clean deck of cards, not a marked, or stacked, deck.

>>Trick 2: *Name calling/mud slinging/ad hominem remarks*—as the various terms suggest individuals in speeches, articles, and books as well as in political and commercial ads will use derogatory epithets to label someone unfavorably. Today these terms have been supplanted by negative attacks and the "politics of destruction." In chapter four we explore further this topic. Some collateral tricks include the use of little and big lies, guilt by headline in the press, and at times the use of straw men, or of anonymous sources to spread rumors.

>>Examples: The use of ethnic, racial, and sexist slurs throughout our history are obvious:

Denotation	Connotation
Jew	kike
Irish	mick
Puerto Rican	spic

woman	whore
Communist	atheist
homosexual	queer

>>Comment: While the first column is usually neutral in simply denoting the term while the second one carries the derogatory connotations, the last two terms are good examples where the denotations and connotations are both heavily laden with emotional overtones. To some Americans, communism represents a utopian dream over the horizon, whereas to other Americans, it represents a living hell as illustrated by the former Soviet Union. Similarly, to some Americans, homosexuality is simply an "alternative life style" while to other Americans it is viewed with distaste and now with foreboding given the spread of AIDS.

As we proceed one technique or trick may slide into another while another trick or concept back tracks or is subsumed by still another. Such is the power and slippery quality of these exercises in persuasion. At times it may appear as if we are in a house of mirrors in a fun house.

Trick 3: *Doomsday enthusiasts or disaster-mongering*—this is an offshoot of card stacking whether in speeches, articles or in book length form. Whether in secular or sectarian terms, this trick asserts that the world is coming to an end, or some particular resource is vanishing.

>>Examples: Aside from religious announcements of the impending apocalypse, the more "popular" ones today have dealt with secular matters:
1 Global warning will lead to the devastation of the earth equivalent to a world wide nuclear war.

2 The world is running out of oil, coal, farmland and other minerals, hence we must undo our profligate ways or face doom. Both items one and two require severe restrictions on our way of life. In turn, these

"necessary changes" plus population control must be mandated by the federal government and the United Nations.

3 The coming world-wide Depression of 2005 will cause suffering to hundreds of millions of people, hence simplify one's life, and buy gold.

>>Comment: In the following chapter on errors of reasoning we allude to this human inclination for simplification and jumping to conclusions. Of course, disaster mongering may mask private motives. "To a greater degree than we often acknowledge, there is appeal for many in the idea that the world will end. The driving force behind it is boredom: The sense that an unending continuation of things would be unendurable, and [hence] the desire for a decisive event…The end of the world is the ultimate great equalizer in which the high are brought low."— Glenn Pascall

>>Trick 4: *transfer* is a process by which either positive or negative associations are moved implicitly or explicitly from one individual to another, from one group to another, from one nation to another.

>>Examples:

1) celebrities selling products, political candidates or community service;
2) professional models doing the same as number one;
3) "plain folks": the use of ordinary people or of professional models that act the "plain folks" part;
4) bandwagon: usually, large crowds of people from number three are utilized suggesting that many or millions cannot be wrong, so come along for the "ride."

>>Comment: Clearly the implied promise in the first two is that success, money and beauty will be conveyed if the product is purchased or

that you will be in good company with "millions" who have bought the product or voted for the candidate. The third appeal is to the contrary impulse that if it is good enough for plain Jim and June then surely it should be good enough for you. Occasionally the bandwagon may utilize celebrities or professionals such as pilots, doctors and other luminaries as pied pipers.

An Abstraction Ladder

High Level Abstraction	**Infinity**
	Earth
	USA
Mid-Level Abstraction	**Washington**
	Seattle
Low-Level Abstraction	**Jane Doe**

>>Trick 5: *Glittering generality or high-level abstraction or platitude*—these are words or phrases that may either soothe or grate on our nerves depending on our point of view. S. I. Hayakawa once called many abstractions "purr" and "snarl" words.

>>Examples:

Truth, Beauty, Goodness
100% American
racism, sexism
the new
youth
communist
atheist

>>Comment: Clearly one person's sparkling platitude is another's act of mud slinging. But the practitioners of propaganda do not move on the imperative to stimulate thought: what they offer are ready made or packaged answers. The few questions that propagandists raise are part and parcel of the *tunneling to a prescribed target*. To that end, they remain in the airy heights of any abstraction ladder.

>>Trick 6: *Bait and switch*—a method by which the gullible are led to believe one thing; or are offered one product; or are offered an inducement; but sadly are shorn like so many sheep when expectations and reality diverge.

>>Examples:

1 The con-artist from folklore is of course the "medicine man" on the frontier offering his magic elixir that cures all ailments for the princely sum of one dollar.

2 Merchants who advertise one product only to inform customers that the aforesaid item has been "sold out" or (sotto voce) "the item is a piece of junk", but then steer the lambs to higher priced merchandise.

3 Bunko artists who offer the elderly the dream of doubling their money in a very brief period of time. One variant scam is to show a "found" wad of cash. Then as a token of good faith to share in the cash, the gullible are led to the banks for withdrawals. Envelopes are swapped; one contains newsprint sliced up to resemble a wad of cash!

4 Real estate come-ons in the swamps of Florida or the deserts of Arizona with very low down payments.

5 Shady tour-operators offering a once in a lifetime trips to Mexico, Hawaii, etc., at a bargain price that vanishes when the gullible arrive at the airport—the operators have vanished with the deposits.

6 Travelogues that are pure card stacking along with travel writers' paeans to paradise without the cockroaches, the mold, stale foods, rotten service, high prices, etc.

>>Comment: Since the seven deadly sins of pride, sloth, lust, envy, gluttony, wrath and avarice are alive and well in human affairs, propagandists are free to choose which human propensity serves their persuasion entree. For the con artist, sparking human greed when combined with flattery of the victim is usually sufficient to close the "deal."

>>Trick 7: *Scapegoating*: perhaps this is as old as the bully picking on the weakest member of the group; or the community running the victim(s) out of town; or the proverbial messenger punished for bringing bad news; or labeling a victim with a Scarlet Letter of "A" for adultery;

or pinning yellow stars of David on Jews in German occupied Europe during the Second World War.
>>Comment: To implement this trick into reality a barrage of card stacking, name-calling, big lies and more are used. After the verbal wars are over, the use of incarceration and force begins. The final step is death.

>>Trick 8: *Mau-mauing*: coercion by actual or implied force in numbers; sometimes mob action.

>>Examples:

1 When a herd of Hells Angels barrels into a sleepy community, a ripple of fear runs rampant.

2 In the late 1960s, the presence of black Panthers on campuses and public building replete with rifles, black leather jackets, and sunglasses.

3 "Student" occupation and thrashing of buildings in 1968 at San Francisco State University and Columbia University.

4 A crowd that storms city hall with its members occupying and thrashing various offices, and then departing by leaving a wake of dead rodents.

5 "Protestors" in Seattle in 1999 at the W.T.O. conference thrashed buildings and stores.

>>Comment: Quite often the image of fear is instilled by the uniform of storm-trooper leather boots and jackets, mean countenance, vile

language and the hint, or show, of weapons, but above all by the menace of sheer numbers and uncertainty.

>>Trick 9: *Equivalence.* For propagandists it is important to obliterate distinctions between molehills and mountains, between degree and kind or, between minor and major matters.

>>Examples:

1 There was no difference between the former USSR and the US—they were both threats to world peace.

2 The US treatment of blacks, American Indians, Japanese-Americans and other minorities is equivalent to the German treatment of the Jews.

3 The US treatment of blacks was no different than that of South Africa before Nelson Mandela became president.

4 Parental spanking of children *is* "child abuse".

5 Banning panhandling and urination in public is a *holocaust* against the poor, the weak, and the uneducated.

>>Comment: Propagandists and advocates of single-issues are enamored by the "isms" of racism, sexism, imperialism, chauvinism, and to an earlier generation the epithet of abuse was nationalism. For those engaged in this trick, *distinctions* must be obliterated.

>>Trick 10: The *shell-game of the "good guys/bad guy"*. This is a favorite short cut of idealists and propagandists uninterested in exploring the underlying causes, incentives, and roles that shape, singly or collectively, individual behaviors.

>>Examples:

1 Americans when confronted with crooked politicians simply advocate "kicking the rascals out" and replacing them with angels.

2 Karl Marx impatient with the growing wealth of merchants and middle class people postulated that the "proletariat" in time would displace these greedy souls and usher in the new utopia and the withering away of the state.

>>Comment: This gamesmanship whether on the local or global level is a variant of black and white or of either/or thinking. The problem of corrupt public officials is often systemic not personal and thus more difficult to eradicate. The other issue of the *creation and distribution* of wealth is often blurred as if one process. A just society of equal incomes without anything to distribute would be an impoverished one.

>>Concept 11: *Stereotyping* involves three definitions:

1) A standardized mental image of people or places;
2) a misleading image or illusion;
3) a preconceived or snap judgment of people or places.

>>Examples: the last one is easily disposed of as we covered it under mud slinging particularly the derogatory ones, hence they are called prejudices. The first one on the other hand may involve a picture say of Switzerland gained from early readings of "Heidi," of yodeling, of cows and mountains. Whether a visit to Switzerland "corrects" this rosy image is a question deferred.

Yet both the movies and television thrive on a stock of stereotypes whether it occurs in Western or police drama. Even if the sound went silent, one could recognize stock characters of the good, the bad and the ugly. In this fashion, viewers draw on the common currency of myths on the prairie and in the asphalt jungle. As entertainment it is one matter. As an instructor it is another.

But the entertainment images can be hazardous to one's health if believed. The good guys do not always triumph; nor is crime always solved by the end of the hour. When coupled with faulty evidence, inappropriate analogies and easy conclusions, the result may lead to vicious stereotypes and violence.

The middle one of a misleading image has many examples. Typically most Americans believe in the pursuit of happiness and that most stories have happy endings. People of other nations smile at our innocence in the face of the daily persistence of evil in the world.

Another American belief that may be a misleading illusion is the notion that all social problems, by definition, have an answer. A collateral part to the foregoing is the notion that it is better to do something even if it does more harm. "Don't just stand there, do something." Unfortunately moving an accident victim may well kill him. In this sanguine viewpoint, good intentions nullify ignorance and incompetence.

>>Comment: "From mass society emerge the psychological elements most favorable to propaganda: symbols and stereotypes...In a mass society, [symbols and stereotypes] are more detached from reality, more manipulable, more numerous, more likely to provoke intense but fleeting emotions, and at the same time less inherent in personal life." —Jacques Ellul

>>Concept 12: *Symbols and signs*: are those words, phrases, and figures that represent something else; a surrogate or stand-in.

>>Examples:

1 figures	Uncle Sam, Miss Liberty
2 people	Washington, Lincoln, Marilyn Monroe, Beatles
3 political	flag, anthem, Constitution

4 places	Wall Street, Main Street, Mt. Rushmore
5 buildings	White House, Lincoln Memorial, Empire State,
6 religion	cross, crescent, Bible, Koran
7 money	$$$$, Yen, Euro
8 success	diamonds, gold, furs, a Rolls
9 labels	enjoy; improved; beautiful; new; you!; now.

>>Comment: As we mentioned above a number of these symbols and signs are also glittering generalities, and of course illustrate the use of transfer. But symbols have the peculiar aspect that they become important and valued for their own sake rather than as a sign of success. Individuals such as the Beatles summarize a turning point in social history. Others such as Marilyn Monroe touch upon fantasies. By forfeiting her life, Monroe gained a permanent place in the company of Olympian goddesses. Earlier James Dean's premature death permitted him to join the celluloid gods of Valhalla.

>>Concept 13: *Euphemism*: the substitution of an inoffensive word or remark for a direct expression; a word of kindness instead of the harsh truth; double-talk.

>>Examples:

1 War Dept.	Defense Dept.
2 retreat	strategic withdrawal
3 undertaker	mortician
4 garbage man	waste hauler
5 toilet	rest room
6 no smoking	extinguish materials
7 airplane	equipment
8 get-off	deplane
9 used car	previously owned

10 bums	homeless
11 died	passed away, expired
12 criminal	juvenile delinquent
13 pregnant	family way
14 AIDS	died of natural causes
15 stupid	exceptional child

>>Comment: in personal affairs, the impulse to be kind is often at war with the need to tell the truth; in political and social affairs, the relabeling creates sympathy for a group that could be considered an "underdog"; but there is a grim side when those in power have something to hide or harm to inflict; the master of these locutions of evasions are of course the totalitarian despots of *1984* that George Orwell so brilliantly depicted. But even in democracies as Orwell also noted politicians are prone to corrupt language to their ends.

>>Concept 14: *Denotation vs. connotation*: we repeat here
the distinction between the neutral, descriptive details of a noun versus its overtones, sometimes heavily freighted with emotions that are either positive or negative.

>>Examples: "Polack…kike, wop, spick, chink, frog, hunky, kraut, slopehead—yes, all these slurs are now far beyond the pale of civilized discourse…We have come
quite a way since the days when newly arrived immigrants and resident minorities fought wars over these words in city streets" as a *Wall Street Journal* editorial recited a history lesson. These slurs are now all politically incorrect.
>>Comment: As this brief catalog has indicated thus far, selected words have power to move us. Often word mongers drop these verbal incendiaries in order to provoke bloodshed.

>>Trick 15: *Color and music*: in of themselves these items are neutral but when used in commercials, political pitches, or public service ads they are background fillers, mood setters, and persuasive emotional clinchers. As noted, they entertain and pull us along in the story line.

>>Examples: as background filler, the *blue* curtain behind politicians before television cameras is ubiquitous; in commercials the pristine qualities of rippling brooks, and mountain greenery are conveyed by transfer to the product; in expensive car ads, the full array of evening clothes, furs, diamonds and nighttime mood plus other winning symbols convey their messages of success with dark colors; as to music, it may be used as an attention grabbing gimmick, punctuation, or as a filler. Or more on MTV.

>>Comment: The use of music, color and line in art hardly requires mention except in an art and music appreciation course; but for the masters of persuasion, music, color and line are means to a given end; what does deserve mention is the institutional obtuseness by managers, administrators and superintendents in the workplace, in hospitals and in schools that have long ignored the "background" color since it affects the productivity of workers, the healing of patients, and the learning by children.

Free Time Activities

WATCH television with a discerning eye and identify as many tricks or techniques of propaganda as you can. Which ones predominate?

WATCH AND LISTEN during election campaigns to speeches and identify as many tricks and techniques of the trade as you can. Is there more than one trick in the repertoire of politicians?

REVIEW IN YOUR MIND'S EYE the press and television news coverage of the Persian Gulf War from August 1990 to March 1991. Was it only news coverage, or were there elements of story telling? Which ones? Similarly, review the Kosovo and Serbian bombing campaigns of the spring of 1999.

WATCH video travelogues and mentally ask what have they left out; also with travel writers' pieces of puffery, similarly ask if this is too good to be true.

READ George Orwell's *1984* for an introduction to "Doublespeak" and "Newspeak" as well as his essay, "Politics and the English Language."

Persuasion Game Notes

Books

J. A. C. Brown, *Techniques of Persuasion: From Propaganda to Brainwashing* (Baltimore: Penguin Books, 1963).

Michael Choukas, *Propaganda Comes of Age* (Washington, D.C.: Public Affairs Press, 1965).

Jacques Ellul, *Propaganda: The Formation of Men's Attitudes* (New York: Alfred A. Knopf,1965), pp. xvii, 94.

Neal Gabler, *Life the Movie* (New York: Alfred A. Knopf, 1998).

George Orwell, *A Collection of Essays*, a Harvest Book, (New York: Harcourt, Brace & Jovanovich, 1981). The essay, "Politics and the English Language" appears on pp. 156–171.

James R. Mock & Cedric Larson, *Words That Won the War: The Committee on Public Information, 1917–1919* (Princeton: Princeton University Press, 1939).

Vance Packard, *The Hidden Persuaders* (New York: David McKay Co., 1957).

Anthony R. Pratkanis & Elliot Aronson, *Age of Propaganda* (New York: W. H. Freeman, 1992).

Alvin A. Snyder, *Warriors of Disinformation* (New York: Arcade Pub. Co., 1995). This work explores the Cold War and the role of the U.S. Information Agency.

Allan M. Winkler, *The Politics of Propaganda: The Office of War Information 1942–1945* (New Haven: Yale University Press, 1978).

Tom Wolfe, *Radical Chic & Mau-Mauing the Flak Catchers* (New York: 1970).

Periodicals

Stephen J. Adler, "Consultants Dope Out The Mysteries of Jurors for Clients Being Sued," *Wall Street Journal*, October 24, 1989, pp. A1, A12 as the author notes that "human behavior is being monitored, dissected and, ultimately, manipulated" by the use of a parallel "jury" for hire. Thus the attorneys can have daily feedback.

E. S. Browning, "The Gallery: Mock Thy Neighbor," *Wall Street Journal*, April 19, 1988, p.26. Browning reviewed an exhibition of French and German political cartoons over the last century that toured both countries. What is clear is the persistence of the symbols and stereotypes by political cartoonists of both countries. Browning observed that "A variety of historians cite opinion polls showing that the French and West Germans have increasingly positive views of each other, suggesting that popular prejudices are disappearing. But the cartoons suggest that they are far from dead."

Cynthia Crossen, "Proliferation of 'Advertorials' Blurs Distinction Between News and Ads," *Wall Street Journal*, April 21, 1988, p.33.

Editorial, *Wall Street Journal*, September 27, 1983, p. 26, on ethnic slurs of the past.

Joanne Lipman, "TV Series on Personal Finance Stirs Debate Over Separation of News and Advertising," *Wall Street Journal*, February 10, 1988, p. 23. One of the tricks of persuasion is to palm off propaganda or advertising as news. Lipman recounts that "a six part series running on the Financial News Network, is actually a three hour commercial" for an insurance company. To make it look like a news program, the series secured the services of a TV network correspondent as host and also paid other reporters from the *New York Times, Forbes*, and *Money Magazine*, at $1,000 each.

William McAllister, "Subtle Pitches: More Business Firms Provide TV Stations with 'News' on Film," *Wall Street Journal*, February 10,1972, pp. 1, 10.

Michael W. Miller, "Seldom is Heard a Discouraging Word: For Travel Writers There's Rarely a Bad Trip when the Hosts are Paying," *Wall Street Journal*, March 18, 1988, pp. D19, D20.

Glenn Pascall, "What Drives the Doomsday Enthusiasts?" Seattle Times, March 13, 1988, p. B1.

Stanley Penn, "Travel Scams," *Wall Street Journal*, March 18, 1988, p. D21.

Virginia Postrel, "The Pleasures of Persuasion," *Wall Street Journal*, August 2, 1999, p. A18. "In our media-savvy age, consumers are neither morons nor puritans. We are active participants in the exchange with producers and persuaders."

Patricia Taylor, "It's Time to Put Warnings on Alcohol," and James C. Sanders, " We Need Role Models, Not Labels," *New York Times*, March 20, 1988, III, p. 2. Read both for the pros and cons of placing warning labels on alcohol.

John Tierney, "Betting the Planet," *New York Times Magazine*, December 2, 1990, pp. 52–53ff. Doomsday prophet Paul Ehrlich lost a ten year bet to Julian Simon that the world would be running out of natural resources.

See Amos Vogel, "Can We Now Forget the Evil that She Did?" *New York Times*, May 13, 1973, II, p. 19, for an exposition and critique of Leni Riefenstahl's 1934 propaganda film for Adolph Hitler, entitled, "Triumph of the Will."

Nicholas Wade, "My Dog Loves Me, and Other Delusions," *New York Times,* July 25, 1999, Section 4, p. 5. On the other hand, NW suggests that many people are credulous and cites dog lovers imputing human qualities to their animals, and the Clever Hans (the horse) gimmick.

Geoffrey Wheatcroft, "'McCarthyism' Is Becoming Orwellian," *Wall Street Journal,* February 9, 2000, p. A26. The author reviews the misuse and overuse today of both terms: McCarthyism and Orwellian.

2

The Game of Errors

What error drives our eyes and ears amiss?

—Shakespeare, *Comedy of Errors*, Act II

In observing the daily human comedy, a collection of errors or fallacies in thinking comes easily to mind. For the most part, these errors, with exceptions, are committed out of stumbling innocence. They represent attempts to impose order on human events by short circuiting what Walter Kaufmann called the aching process by which we seek to understand the world we inhabit. The following errors take place when individuals often ignore facts, twist arguments, and draw conclusions that may be comforting but fallacious. One might say that these errors facilitate our vulnerability to easy persuasion. Thus these errors are corollaries to the tricks of chapter one. Therefore, the reader is cautioned to beware of the siren call of short cuts in reasoning as this brief compendium of two dozen plus illustrates.

To begin with, consider the following catalog with its *fallacies of reasoning*: the human propensity is to explain the unexplainable; or to take shortcuts; or to engage in puffery. At times these mental errors by individuals flow from lack of education, thought and laziness. When *deliberately* practiced by advertisers, spin-doctors of public relations and special interests' propaganda they join the arsenal of persuasion tricks cited at the outset.

>>1 *Jumping to conclusions*: in terms of baseball, it is as if the runner decides to run to third instead of to first base as the rules demand; this mental shortcut is common, the wish to express an opinion on any subject, for example, the reporter at the scene of an airplane crash surmises that the crash occurred because of wind-shear; or the desire to act, without any facts, experience, statistics, study or expert testimony; stereotyping would be another name for this vagrant activity.

"Also a good way to identify a bum."

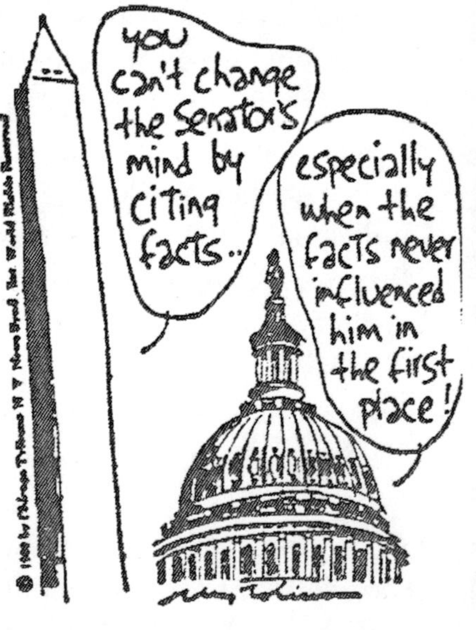

>>2 *Fallacy of composition*: mistaking what is true for the part, to be true also for the whole; what is good for GM is good for the US; what is good for Susie Jones is good for everyone; what is good for Washington State is good for the entire country; needless to say, the reverse may be equally fallacious that what is good for the whole is good for the part.

>>3 *Either/or fallacy*: reducing all issues to a two dimensional plane by removing all shades of gray and in-betweens to an over-simplification; a kindred spirit to jumping to conclusion: "if you're not for us, you're against us!"; "if you are not for communism, you are a fascist!"

>>4 *Begging the question*: calling for a conclusion in the guise of being impartial, a favorite of criminal lawyers: "Is it true that you have stopped beating your wife?" No matter how you answer this booby trap, you are doomed. Another example, a citizen's committee decides that "This *unjust* tax should be repealed and we will *research* the matter." Here the conclusion or the "fix" is in before the so-called research is done. Again a variant of jumping to conclusion.

>>5 *Straw man*: the creation of an imaginary opponent; or the use of the collective "we vs. they"; or at times, the dead are chosen for their inability to reply; or a non-existent reliable "source".

>>6 *Perry Mason technique*: planting an irrelevant question in the jury's mind to discredit a hostile witness. Although overruled, the question lingers: "Were you not in a mental institution in 1999?"

>>7 *Pathetic fallacy* occurs when one ascribes human qualities or feelings to inanimate things, events, or processes: "Screaming headline," "cruel depression," "Hurricane Edna." But the harm caused by these stale metaphors may be minimal. Otherwise daily speech would be correct but drab without the metaphors.

>>8 *Ignoring the question* or issue:

a by asking another question;
b by smearing your opponent, or interviewer, or debater;
c by shifting to another topic;
d by asking for the same question again, smiling, and saying, "I thought so, may I have the next question;"
e by walking away; ending the interview or by pooh-poohing a debater.

>>9 *Equivocation*: substituting one abstraction for another, unwittingly; if wittingly then it is an attempt to stall, to dodge the issue or question: "Capital punishment is not the issue, the condition of the homeless is the proper question." "Liberty is not the issue, equality is."

>>10 *Venus Syndrome*: the egotistical notion that only your voice fills the universe and when the voice ceases, the universe will fall into a black hole; also known as *solipsism*, the notion that the self is the only reality; when a few such souls unite into one dissonant screech others would do well to find a soundproof shelter.

>>11 *Seeing is believing*: an ancient error whether it be the examples of the desert shimmer of water; the train tracks that meet; the sun that rises and falls; the eye-witness who swears by the light of the moon what he saw (even when there was no moonlight that night); in short the caution that appearances may be deceiving, or things are not at times what they seem.

>>12 *Conspiracies everywhere*: this is a another version of seeing is believing; the propensity to believe that some secret group is pulling the strings of human affairs; for those prone to jumping to conclusions: large scale social disruptions such as war and depressions are likely to

be explained by the workings of the Zionist Jews, the CIA, the Mafia, or the Trilateral Commission. For those who once found Moscow to be the Holy Grail, the United States remained the arch-Satan, especially the government, the source of all evil in the world. Needless to say this perspective fits a number of the above fallacies. Quite often others misconstrue a *conjunction* of interests (by individuals or groups) as a conspiracy.

>>13 *Experience vs. book learning*: according to this view, what people learn from daily experience in the school of hard knocks is much more effective than book and school learning. Benjamin Franklin had a retort to this either/or fallacy when he noted, "Experience keeps a dear school, yet fools will learn in no other."

>>14 *Practice vs. theory*: [a variant of number 13 above] the notion that theory is impractical knowledge dreamed up by some absent minded professor; as when someone says, "it's OK in theory, but not in practice"; whereas the pursuit of the practical, what works is what is required; another either/or situation that misconstrues what a theory truly encompasses.

>>15 *Non-sequitur*: from the Latin meaning it does **not** follow from an initial observation, point, or premise; *if, then* arguments that are known as hypothetical syllogisms are often misused not unlike "theory" and "analogies."

a Two men are observed standing at a bus stop, the police arrest the two for engaging in a drug transaction. Barring further evidence, the two were simply standing at the bus stop.

b If we can put a man on the moon, then why can't we eliminate...[fill in your favorite social cause]? (Recognize the trick of equivalence?)

c If we can spend billions of dollars on gum and cosmetics and underarm deodorants, then why can't we spend more money on...[again fill in]?
d If it's not on the TV news, then it didn't happen.
e If science can't measure it, then it can't be too important an issue.
f If an aspect of teaching can't be measured, even if it exists, then it can't be too important.
g If it's on television, then it must be true!

>>16 *Nolo contendere*: again from the Latin, it means "no contest"; in civil court, the defendant may so plead thereby neither admitting nor denying responsibility; in arguments, it means that there is no meeting of minds; one participant may be metaphorically on the 44th floor while the other party is on the 10th floor. Also faulty or false information leads to no contest, no solution, and no transaction. Walter Lippmann cites a classic case: "A man may have the finest automobile, be the best driver, have perfect vision and a heart of gold. But if he tries to find his way around Paris with a map of Chicago...he will not arrive where he set out to go."

>>17 *Confusing tastes* (private affairs) of hobbies and life style with *competence* (work ethic). The latter includes training, experience, technical skills, initiative, attitudes of punctuality and reliability, etc.

>>18 *Praise the exception to the detriment of the rule* or social norm: crime is the daily rule, but the perception by the general public is that criminals (as the rule) receive undue care and protection of their rights. All to the detriment of the wrongs inflicted upon victims and society whose pain and suffering are viewed as exceptions. The media elite pooh-poohs the level of crime and the judicial system fosters a revolving door of criminal conduct. We have another example of the social fallacy of composition?

>>19 *Confusing changes in degree with a change in kind*: a) when water at sea level changes its state at 32 and 212 degrees; b) when caterpillars change into butterflies; c) social processes and turning points: on the one hand we are informed that "things will get worse before they get better." On the other hand we are told to ignore the issue, not to give it any recognition, thereby hastening its departure. For example, parents of teenagers today are rightfully concerned when drugs are involved and whether their children are sincere and willing to forgo further use of drugs. But at some point, the youngsters may go over the edge by overdosing. Should parents wait or intervene early?
On a different level, there are the costly military programs that require more and more funds to no avail because the prototype does not work. Having spent billions, the political process is hesitant to scrap the program as a failure. Still another example occurs when a successful small business stumbles over expansion. Five stores are manageable but twenty-five stores overwhelms the mind-set of a small businessman. Finally, the normal growth of children that appears imperceptible to parents but to aunts and uncles visiting on birthdays, and holidays the changes in kind are duly noted and applauded.

>>20*Fallacy of double and triple counting*: a variant of card stacking: "The poor, the elderly, blacks, and women require a crash program to eliminate poverty in the country." Obviously an individual could be a black, a woman, poor and elderly as well. But the sentence multiplies the situation by four for political effect.

>>21 *Fallacy of there is no tomorrow* or time can wait or be discounted: this is the gambling instinct that prefers quick payoffs rather than planning for the future; some would insist that this is a matter of taste or values rather than a misleading stance on personal and social issues; but tomorrow comes with its own consequences for both individuals and society that choose to ignore the march of time.

>>22 *Fallacy* of the *ad hoc* or pragmatism revisited: in political terms this means an obsession with current details to the exclusion of any long-run considerations, any side effects, any inter-relationships of issues; in short, what will work, *now*; even if it is a band-aid approach to social and political issues.
Speaking of John F. Kennedy as president, Walt W. Rostow, one of his advisers, hailed him as "a pragmatist." David Marquand noted however "The essence of the pragmatic approach to politics is to avoid the long-term forecasts, and to deal with events piecemeal, as they occur." But Marquand adds that pragmatism places intellectual blinders on its adherents while "details are meaningless in themselves; and only 'philosophic musing' can give them significance." Which means that politicians always trail the electorate on social changes and issues until various crises explode into public consciousness.
Of course during the so-called campus revolts in the late 1960s, the slogans of "Now" and "Relevance" and other catch phrases served as incantations and as siblings of the ad hoc. Such radicals were seemingly under the impression that they had transcended the culture of their mentors and fathers.

>>Comment: "...it is not enough for our rulers and administrators who hold the world in their hands, to have no more than an ordinary intelligence, no more ability than us. They are very much below if they are not very much above us. As they promise more, so they owe more." —Montaigne

>>23 *Self-fulfilling prophecy*: a situation where one repeats and repeats a certain prediction and thus contributes in whole or in part towards its fulfillment:

a when a parent repeatedly informs a son that he will amount to no good, and the son obliges;
b when a spouse berates the other but never praises only to be surprised by a "divorce".
c one prophecy that did **not** happen: social critics who insisted that the major cities of the country would have endless summer riots beyond the 1960s, in one form or another; of course these urban upheavals came to a close, no doubt, in part because of the law of diminishing marginal rage.

>>24 *"Patriotism as the last refuge of the scoundrel,"* so averred Samuel Johnson. In short, patriotism provides the shield of public virtue behind which particular private interests flourish.

a *National defense* is a favorite of politicians and private businessmen seeking some privilege, or dispensation. Often a community will resist the closing of a military base on "national defense" grounds. This is the reverse of the NIMBY (Not in My Back Yard) syndrome.
b *A level playing field* is a favorite metaphor of politicians and their clients: industries and unions seeking protective tariffs and quotas. International trade takes place because production costs *differ*. At the turn of the century, the favorite metaphor for protection was a

"scientific tariff" which sought the same end, to stop trade, to deny consumers and businesses choices and to reduce standards of living.

c *Fair trade pricing* is another favorite metaphor of politicians and domestic manufacturers intent on rigging prices for small appliances. These unfair practices flourished after World War Two and were eventually repealed to the delight of consumers shopping at discount stores.

d End pollution and global warning immediately! Planet Earth is in the balance!

>>Comment: Who is in favor of *Japanese interests*? Who is in favor of *uneven playing fields*? Who is in favor of *unfair prices*? Or *unfairness* in general? Who is in favor of polluted environments? What these examples suggest is that many public policies (that benefit the few at the expense of the many) are sold just like private products with misleading slogans, symbol manipulation, and Orwellian doublespeak.

>>25 *100 per cent Syndrome*: the belief that perfection by individuals and institutions in society can/should be achieved; the collateral premise that all "problems" in human affairs have "solutions;" an all or nothing stance.

a End population pollution by all means available! Zero population growth must be implemented immediately.

b The United Way promoter who insists on 100% employee payroll deductions.

c The union leader who calls for 100% union membership in a given plant or office.

d The pundits who call for 100% voter turnouts as a mark of effective citizenship.

e The educational critic who calls for no high school drop-outs; 100% of students must graduate.

f The belief that what people say, they do (on December 31st countless individuals make New Year's resolutions only to break them shortly thereafter).

g Religious calls for total abstention of drink, smoking and other sins of the flesh.

h The death row lawyer's assertion that since the judicial system is imperfect, capital punishment ought to be abolished.

i Environmentalists who insist that pollution of air and water must be reduced 100 %.

j Artificial sweeteners, food additives, and coloring agents must be 100% safe or done away with.

k Organ transplants should not be performed unless they are 100% safe.

l Nuclear power plants must not be used unless they are 100% safe; the same with nuclear wastes.

m New pharmaceutical drugs must not be introduced until they are 100% safe.

n A zero-tolerance policy towards drug use.

>>Comment: Not too long ago in our culture, an excellent attendance record (zero absences) in school and on the job was esteemed; but today both workers and students when not ill are absent for reasons of pleasure, medical reasons and family emergencies. However, many of the above positions cited are no doubt sincerely held by many, but they ignore trade-offs and social frictions in human, biological and physical realms. For want of safe drugs, people die. By placing off-limits an Alpine lake's rusticity from public use, many are denied its delights. Ironically the call for the immediate shut-down of nuclear plants and hydro dams to save salmon leads to greater use of fossil fuel plants with greater acid rain effusions, higher accident rates and contributions to global warming!

As to closet communists and kindred spirits, Irving Howe has sketched those aspects of individual feelings that hunger for perfection and at times find a home by total surrender to the idea of communism and its surrogate, the former Soviet Union. From the closets there emerged a number of traitors in the United States and Great Britain. What are these qualities that the true believers hunger for? Howe outlines the following three items:

1) "a feeling of having brought into active engagement a larger portion of one's moral energies than routine life allows; 2) a sense of inner harmony, in the past achieved through religious experience or romantic intuitions of nature, but now to be had through political activity; 3) a subordination of ego to purpose, small vanity to large end, individual personality to collective structure." Howe adds "What is interesting about any such listing of the parts of 'wholeness' is that it runs the gamut from the morally best to the worst, from a wish for authenticity to a hunger for submission." The latter runs the further danger of the totalitarian temper in which all means are mete for the unleashing of the coming utopia. In this scenario, people, sadly, not just eggs will be broken on the quest for social perfection.

>>26 *Calling the game off*: "It's my ball, and if you won't play by my rules I'll go home." A variant on a smaller scale of the Venus Syndrome. Demonstrations, protests and fire-bombings are utilized that seek to stop the airing of viewpoints in public speeches and debates that protesters abhor. Only "our" views are politically correct. The WTO conference in Seattle in November 1999 comes to mind.

Still another example of this intransigence involves high school students who prefer to play the game of writing by their rules. English teachers across the land have the thankless task of improving student writing. Yet, the cardinal assumption by many students is that *thought and writing are divorced*. Hence the raised eyebrows when teachers red-pencil student compositions. Hart Leavitt, a long-suffering reader of student prose, took pen in hand to delineate the seven deadly sins of teen-age compositions:

1) *Pretentious diction*: huffing and puffing instead of the "right word at the right time";
2) *Idiotic idiom*: following grammatical rules that lead to wooden prose;
3) *Burnt-out sentence ends*: weak sentences with dangling and loose ends; no punch line;
4) *Poor relations*: misuse of conjunctions to show cause and effect; also, no movement up and down the abstraction ladder;
5) *No contest:* student "compositions will go on being dull as long as students write on dull subjects;"
6) *Padded sell*: a cousin to the first above in using glittering generalities;
7) *The big think*: generalizations without specifics; jumping to conclusions.

>>27 *Stonewalling any problem solving*. Just as there are errors of thinking, so there are deliberate means of forestalling action on countless issues that clutter the public agenda. Public officials and the media may choose to:
1 *Ignore* the problem
2 *Deny* the existence of the problem.
3 *Recognize* the problem solely.
4 *Define* it away.
5 *Study* it with a blue ribbon panel.
6 *Schedule endless hearings* and meetings.
7 *Bury* it in a barrage of abstractions.
8 *Solve* partially.
9 *Do nothing* citing lack of funds.
10 *Displace* the old with a new problem.
>>Comment: of course these devices of stalling could just as well be placed in chapter three. However if the problems are political, some of the above tactics may be legitimate. Even desirable social programs must face

the limits of resources: money, time, and manpower that must be allocated for some, while denying resources for other, programs.

To conclude our brief catalog of errors, we turn to the original critic of lapsed ways of thinking. Francis Bacon (1561–1626) in his four *idols of the mind* took on some of the mental detours that we have introduced here and in our initial chapter. In *idols of the tribe*, Bacon deftly punctured the human propensity to believe only what we see; to leap to conclusions on flimsy or no evidence; and finally to reject ideas that jar our preconceptions. One has only, for example, to present the stimuli of glittering generalities or purr words and the mind opens; present the converse and the mind snaps shut.

In *idols of the cave*, he cautioned us against the true believers, the special pleaders, as well as those experts who know more and more about less and less. A current example would be "experts" who engage in card stacking as "hired guns" of special interests. Of course, true believers of any cause would overlap these last two classifications. If Bacon were alive today, he would recognize immediately the countless singe-issue organizations with their finely honed card stacking literature. Many of the issues of global warming, ozone depletion, save the salmon, abortion, abolishing the death penalty, shutting down nuclear plants, and environmental purity would be new to him, but the techniques of persuasion utilized in these causes would be quite familiar if not old-hat.

In the *idols of the marketplace,* Bacon was aware of the glitter attendant to generalities that strain for the blue sky bereft of earthly details. Also he observed the human itch to short-circuit thinking by using labels, slogans and stereotypes. The latter in part could be pre-cooked conclusions that elicited knee-jerk responses from the converted. Lastly in the *idols of the theater*, he noted the siren call of all enveloping systems and dogma as well as the seductions of a deductive reasoning without a grounding in details, facts and experiences. Yet these mental dead-ends, these closed systems can provide solace, an anchor, and the company of other shivering souls as Irving Howe above indicated. Clearly the idols of the tribe and the theater are emotional cousins. On this aspect more in chapter five.

Above all, Bacon had an unerring instinct that card stacking is the paramount technique of persuasion. Bacon noted that once an individual adopts an opinion, he then "draws all things else to support and agree with it." Even though other opinions and facts are available, Bacon went on to insist, the individual "neglects and despises, or by some distinction sets aside and rejects; in order that by this great and pernicious predetermination the authority of its former conclusions may remain inviolate." Thus "*pernicious predetermination*" was the card stacking of Bacon's time.

Free Time Activities

READ newspaper editorials, opinions and letters to the editors and discover as many errors of reasoning as you can. Is there a major error that is popular? Why is it used so often?

LOOK at television news and note if reporters are adding opinions and commentary without labeling as such and what errors of thinking they are using. Do the reporters nod in agreement to their own questions?

LISTEN to radio talk shows and itemize the popular errors of reasoning, especially from the hosts of the shows.

Game of Errors Notes

Books

Periodicals

Clare Ansberry, "Calling Sexes Equal in Domestic Violence, Article Stirs Clash Among Rights Groups," *Wall Street Journal*, May 5, 1988, p. 29. One person's article of faith is another's example of jumping to conclusions. Ansberry's article illustrates this well.

William M. Carly, "In a Big Plane Crash, Cause Probably Isn't Everybody's Guess," *Wall Street Journal*, March 29, 1988, pp. 1, 21. An excellent article illustrating the rush to judgment or jumping to conclusion in the media's handling of airplane crashes.

John Ciardi, "Manner of Speaking: Analogy and Mind," *Saturday Review*, June 9, 1962, p. 20. Ciardi speaks of the 100 per centers as all or nothing proponents: "They are the zealots, and they are the barbarians we breed within our own gates."

Gar Anthony Haywood, "They Were Wrong, but I'm Glad They Asked," *Seattle Times*, January 24, 1988, pp. K1,K2 is a classic case of jumping to conclusion: neighbors hear the screams of two infant children, ergo, child abuse, hence a call to the police. The police came, saw, and left. Haywood concluded that "with time I came to understand that all too often the truths seen by the naked eye turns out to be lies. Smiles hide demons, and warmth masks madness. External appearances and perfectly rational explanations cannot always be trusted. Clearly, then, the overzealous neighbor who had blown the whistle had acted on the only concrete evidence that she had: the semi-regular cries of a child." This particular child was a screamer for all occasions.

Irving Howe quoted in "Notable and Quotable," *Wall Street Journal*, May 12, 1978, p.18.

Hart Leavitt, "The Seven Deadly Sins of Teen-age Composition," *Scholastic Magazine*, March 15, 1961.

David Marquand, "The Pragmatic Liberal," *Manchester Guardian*, February 6, 1964.

The Walt Rostow quote appears in Harvey Cox, *The Secular City* (New York: Macmillan, 1965), p.62.

Thomas H. Sowell, "People are Dying for Safety's Sake," *Seattle Times*, March 11, 1985, p. A12, decries the impulse for "perfect solutions."

3

The Ad Game

> ...the poet's role [is] to give the facts of everyday existence a meaning beyond itself...The advertiser, usurping the poetic function does the same...
>
> —S. I. Hayakawa

From coast to coast has cultural illiteracy spread like a laser beam? According to recent surveys, young and old betray an ignorance of Beowulf, Chaucer, Spenser, Dante, Shakespeare, Keats, Tennyson, Goethe and Frost? Are they new rock musicians, or what? If not, who cares?

Into the breach have come the jingles, jangles and slogans of Madison Avenue supplemented by the music-videos of MTV cold-hustling hot CDs.

Are these the new poets of the age? The up-front faces with the back-room practitioners of percussive music, color, strobe lights, sound, and symbols? Do we have high-tech poetry, spliced and sliced selling new and old products, people, and ideas?

From Elvis to the Beatles, from Chubby Checkers to Bob Dylan, and from the Rolling Stones to Madonna and Michael Jackson, are these the new "artists" of the imagination? If Neal Gabler is right, these "artists" are but bit players in our own daily "movie". But they exemplify selling as entertainment.

To begin with, poor nations rarely require the services of advertisers whether they offer high-tech or old-tech techniques. Those without income do not need advice on how to spend. But affluence and advertising go hand in hand. More often than not, advertising rides on the wave of economic growth and its resultant increases in material well-being. In short, we have a positive-sum game with winners in varying degrees.

Yet economists for the most part take a dim view of the role of advertising. They do so not out of pique but rather from the perspective that advertisers are engaged in a shell game of selling more of one good at the expense of another seller. In short, GM's loss is, Ford's, or the Japanese's, gain. Here we have a zero-sum game with winners and losers.

Economists concede that when advertising *informs* rather than *persuades* it provides a useful function for consumers. By providing information, consumers can act intelligently or more rationally. What type of ad would fit this bill? We are all familiar with the weekly food specials and variety store ads that list specials by price and number. These ads perform a clear function for the consumer in conserving time by announcing where the goods are, at what price, and when they are available.

Yet modern advertising is likely to succeed when it persuades under the guise of informing the customer as when a truly new product is introduced as opposed to another brand of an existing product. Step by step, the announcement of the new product leads to the alleged void in the consumers' life just as a bathtub must be filled. As Jacques Ellul has noted of this process: "New needs are created from the day a new product appears. After a few months of getting used to a product, its absence will be felt because an effective need will have been created. But the need was created exclusively by advertising."

However advertising agencies and their clients have long ignored this distinction between announcement and persuasion. Why? In part because in our affluent society, many final consumer goods and services are so *similar* as to be indistinguishable. Thus the appointed task of modern advertising is to sell goods by indirection, less on the merits, than of consumer emotional needs to be satisfied if brand x rather than brand y is purchased.

As one advertiser noted that "You have to sell on emotion more than ever because it's a world of parity products out there." Parity is the euphemism for similar products. For the most part, the intrinsic qualities of automobiles, VCRs, tires, tennis racquets, hair dryers, perfumes, and jeans are non-existent to the consumer.

For example, if the same Singapore seamstress sews on various labels, the price will vary according to the "designer labels" attached, not to the garment, itself. It is this realm of snob-appeal and symbolic add-on that draws the ire of economists. Advertising raises the price of goods two ways, by the direct cost of advertising and the added psychic price. Should economists object if consumers wish to be flimflammed? Moreover in a democracy and in a free marketplace, consumers have a right to pursue their own road to happiness.

But economists are consistent. Along with their opposition to the unnecessary role of modern advertising, they object for similar reasons to gambling in any guise or manner. For the losses of some, are the gains of others, in other words, another zero-sum game. As a result no new economic activity has been created, just a switch of funds. Surely Las Vegas and Atlantic City create jobs? But they are incidental to the transfer of funds from one party to another. To economists, the workers at these gambling casinos would be employed more productively elsewhere.

Despite these criticisms, advertising since the 1920s appears secure in its modern role of targeting psychological needs rather than physical wants. Advertising today moves on a few simple propositions about human nature. Initially, the consumer is assumed *not* to know the difference, if any, between and within categories of goods; secondly that the consumer will not consult consumer publications for ratings of goods and services; thirdly that the consumer is as likely to buy on impulse expensive durable goods, including homes, as inexpensive tooth paste; fourthly that despite consumer skepticism of ads in general, consumers will buy by brand name. Given the foregoing assumptions, advertisers have a license to move consumers from one queue to another.

As to the tools of advertising, the preceding chapter serves as a useful introduction. But in addition to dividing ads as to whether they inform or persuade, a still more useful distinction is between those messages that promise us an *exchange* versus those that *lecture* to us. The former asks the consumer to part with cash or credit in return for a product or service (or the voter is asked to vote for candidate X in exchange for his services); or a citizen is asked to donate to a worthy cause in return for the glow of compassion. In these exchanges, a *quid pro quo* is clear. On the other hand, there are ads that hector or harangue us to *stop* certain personal behaviors: forest fires, littering, smoking, unsafe sex, the spread of AIDS, drug addiction and other public nuisances. Needless to say the latter group of public service ads are neither profitable nor as easily accomplished as selling beer and soft drinks.

Then there are those institutional ads that offer neither a transaction nor a lecture, but are attempts to ingratiate the company or agency as a warm, caring, corporation with a social conscience. By indirection, the ads ask us to think well of Boeing, the Red Cross, the United Way, and the Big Apple. Then there are business firms that do not sell retail goods but are engaged in the production of intermediate or capital goods, yet they court public goodwill. These would include machine goods, steel companies and construction firms engaged in building industrial plants, factories and office towers. Hence they are anxious that their corporate logos enter public consciousness. On public television, business firms are restricted to showing their logos and to succinct messages or mini-ads.

Given this introduction, how does advertising go about its appointed task of persuasion? To begin with, Figure l illustrates a simplified spectrum of persuasion with the two classic poles of carrot and stick. To be sure, advertisers

Punishment <——————————————————> Rewards

Figure 1

do not have the power to punish consumers who disobey their siren calls, but they can suggest that those who fail to heed its messages will not be part of the social bandwagon. Failing to rub soap flakes with the beautiful people, they will be banished to the land of the ugly. Banishing pain can also be profitable as when pain killer commercials promise to rid those metaphorical hammers on the anvil of the brain. Now, our simple spectrum can be redrawn to conform more closely to the range of devices in the marketplace of persuasion. In Figure 2, we note that while advertisers may suggest punishment if the product in question is not purchased, most advertisers will clothe their messages on the right side of the spectrum. To move leftward is to suffer diminishing degrees of success.

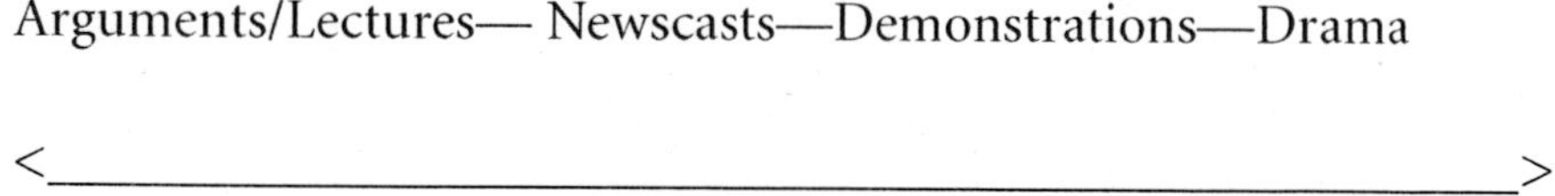

<——————————————————————————>

Punishments Rewards

Figure 2

We shall treat both drama and demonstration as rewards because they candy-coat as so many M&Ms the message with the two oldest genres of: *tell me a story*, and *show me*. Both genres overlap and are often present in television and radio ads. But even ads on the printed page reveal this marriage of forms. Increasingly, interviewing the man on the street, or presenting polls on the popularity of the product being pushed utilizes the device of pseudo-newscast. Here the trick is to mask persuasion as information and thus offer a backhanded tribute to the criticisms of economists. This is a good illustration of our earlier observation that persuasion often works best in disguise.

But the minute we move left of center, advertisers run into a severe barrier not unlike a sound barrier. To be sure the full-page ad, for instance, featuring nothing but arguments extolling the virtues of a Mercedes is an anomaly. No doubt the makers of the ad assume that those who can afford the car have the income, education and willingness to read these ads. But this is questionable. Why? For time itself is a scarce commodity in an affluent society.

More typically, a full-page ad listing the pros and cons of a social issue, or a comparison of brand x and y is seen as something to be avoided or as a "duty" bordering on punishment. For the most part, advertisers are willing to take human nature as it is rather than remold it. So reason must take a holiday while emotions are caressed. The appeal is not to balance contending impulses and interests but rather to satisfy immediate emotional needs. For emotional engineering, the curriculum is never far from the *seven deadly sins* of pride, envy, gluttony, sloth, covetousness, anger, and lust. So the appeals go forward to be "first", to join the bandwagon, to imitate the successful and to pick from the menu of our appetites.

However as an introduction and crash course to our culture, the influence of advertising has not been given its due. With polyglot communities of newcomers to our shores, the old notion that the public schools would acculturate much less melt the new arrivals into mainline Americans, must give way to the daily and tireless instructors on how to spend their money. Newcomers become American consumers before becoming citizens. But advertising agencies and their clients are not directly interested in this sociological dividend that is a valuable cultural and political by-product.

Like robots, the televised commercials do not tire in their repetition. Why does modern advertising hammer away and repeat itself? Ellul reminds us that the consumer must not be permitted the luxury of recovering from the daily bombardment nor remain untouched. Above all, to take hold in the consumer's consciousness the ads require time. But technology today grants the viewer the veto of the remote control. "Zapping" TV ads appears increasingly pervasive.

In general, advertisers rely on a trio of gimmicks, genres, and other devices to lure buyers to their wares of the moment. The proverbial pretty woman, scantily clad, has been an enduring gimmick or attention grabber even if unrelated to the product at hand. But if the gimmick can be related and made an integral part of the product so much the better. The particular devices that compose an ad will be discussed shortly.

Penetrating our homes, television permits not only the full panoply of symbolic manipulations and tricks mentioned above, but also the advantages of motion, music, and color. Color obviously has its own logic of persuasion from the somber to the cheerier hues, from the status tones of richness to the businesslike blues. Even the printed page sans motion and music can convey the powers of color from the whiskey ads to the ordinary colors of margarine and salad dressing ads.

Curiously, on television, ads and programs (including newscasts) constitute a series of sandwiches with the ads as the cold cuts and the programs as the bread. It is the ads that utilize the medium and push it to its limits with split screens, voice-overs and other technical devices. Most ads value time. By contrast the entertainment programs and TV newscasts inhabit an earlier age and are prolific in their waste of time.

On the printed page, the ad must stop the natural human reflex of turning the page. Hence the need for a gimmick whether it be the aforesaid attractive model or an empty page. Once momentarily delayed, the eye must be led by visible or invisible planes to move diagonally or perpendicularly to the message, the product, or the demonstration. Or, for example, a sylvan background of waterfall and green forest can serve many products from cold beer to cigarettes.

In fact anyone with scissors and paste can produce a simple mental or manual test by cutting out particular products and superimposing them on different backgrounds. Or an existing ad may have its elements re-arranged. It is a simple but rewarding exercise. Sometimes colors when not used as a gimmick or filler may be used as a contrast or even as an integral part of the emotional appeal to pride or envy. To splash on color is to bathe an ad.

Needless to say this splashing of color is selective to the extent that consumers are kept in a buying mood. Yet these efforts border on something else. Professor S. I. Hayakawa once observed that it was "the poet's role to give the facts of everyday existence a meaning beyond itself." Where does this lead? "The advertiser, usurping the poetic function," Hayakawa continued, "does the same...whiskey becomes a symbol of adventure. Cigarettes, blankets, Coca-Cola, toothpaste, are surrounded with all kinds of symbols: happiness, gaiety, romance—nothing but poetizing." Today fashion and style reign everywhere in the products of our dreams.

Since these words were uttered consumer tastes and attitudes have shifted dramatically particularly toward hard liquor and cigarettes. So much so that the latter is a candidate for an endangered products list given the tobacco litigation and increased tobacco taxes.

Despite these shifts, the advertisers' work remains. Of necessity, advertisers resort to card stacking by presenting the sunny aspect of life. "There are areas of emotion it dares not touch," Hayakawa observed, "sacrifice, responsibility, hard work and other-worldliness." Ellul agrees that "A propaganda that stresses virtue over happiness and presents man's future as one dominated by austerity and contemplation would have no audience." However, politicians have been known to gingerly broach these last mentioned personal and civic virtues.

Do the "hidden persuaders" of Madison Avenue have unlimited powers to manipulate us against our will? Are there no limits? Indeed there are despite the notion that the "black arts" of propaganda are but a step away from brainwashing. First of all, all forms of persuasion are likely to succeed it they go with the grain of existing attitudes and preconceptions. Secondly, the persuader whatever his kit bag of tricks cannot like King Canute hold back basic economic and social trends in the society. As Ellul observes "Propaganda is definitely not an arsenal of ready-made valid techniques and arguments, suitable for use everywhere." Thirdly, propaganda must build its case on selective facts and hurry along to its conclusion for action. Fourthly, the persuasion must be continuous otherwise it melts away like an ice cube on a hot day. Persuasion must be pervasive and repetitive. Lastly the product must ultimately sell itself. Junk may fool some customers initially, but eventually junk will be found out for what it is. Subject to these limitations, and they are considerable, the persuaders hearken to their trade.

Free Time Activities

1 *LOOK* at television ads: identify and count the number of tricks of persuasion present.

2 *READ* newspaper and magazine ads: identify as many tricks of the trade. Also note how the eye is guided either by color, design, print or other means to move in a specified direction.

3 *MENTALLY* rearrange a selection of printed ads by layout or color to improve their impact. Or cut and paste parts from several ads into a new one.

4 Which *genre* predominates in television ads, which in printed ads? Which on billboards? Which on MTV?

Ad Game Notes

Books

Jacques Ellul, *Propaganda, op. cit.*, pp. 40,34.

Jackson Lears, *A Cultural History of Advertising in America* (New York: Basic Books, 1994).

Periodicals

Ronald Alsop, "Advertisers Struggle to Portray Subject of Death in Commercials," *Wall Street Journal*, January 27, 1988, p. 23.

Ronald Alsop, "Ads That Make Fun of Ads Are In, As Firms Face a More Jaded Buyer," *Wall Street Journal*, February 22, 1988, p.21.

Ronald Alsop, "Advertisers Put Consumers on the Couch," *Wall Street Journal*, May 13, 1988, p. 19.

Ernest Beck, "Ad Bans Abroad [Norway, Finland and Canada] Haven't Snuffed Out Smoking," *Wall Street Journal*, June 12, 1997, pp. B1, B13.

Bruce Charlton, "How Hitler Tried to Stub Out Smoking," *London Times*, July 7, 1994, p. 17.

Laurie P. Cohen, "Sex in Ads Becomes Less Explicit, As Firms Turn to Romantic Images," *Wall Street Journal*, February 11, 1988, p. 25.

Amitai Etzioni, "Human Beings Are Not Very Easy to Change After All, "*Saturday Review*, June 3, 1972, pp. 45–47.
Daniel Harris, "Making Kitsch from AIDS," *Harper's*, July 1994, pp. 55–60.

S. I. Hayakawa's comments on advertisers as poets are quoted by Robert Alden in his column in the *New York Times*, December ll, 1960, III, p. 14.

Dennis Kneale, "'Zapping' of TV Ads Appears Pervasive," *Wall Street Journal*, April 25, 1988, p.27.

Holman W. Jenkins Jr., "The Customer Isn't Always Right," *Wall Street Journal*, June 23, 1999, p. A27. Reviews Coke scare in Belgium as well as Tylenol, and Audi customer complaints in the U.S.

Michael J. McCarthy, "Mind Probe," *Wall Street Journal*, March 22, 1991, p. B3. Ads that work "are candid-camera testimonials, ads that offer solutions to a problem, and product demonstrations." Why do they work? "Although mundane, such approaches are appealing because they present information in a way that doesn't tax a viewer's brain."

Dana Milbank, "Being a Consumer Isn't Easy if You Boycott Everything," *Wall Street Journal*, April 24, 1991, p. 1. A summary of extremists who shun many products on environmental and political grounds.

Robin Pogrebin, "By Design or Not, an Ad Becomes a Fad," *New York Times*, Section 4, December 24, 1995, p. 3. "Teen-agers around the country are collecting the colorful, clever advertisements for Absolut Vodka that appear in glossy magazines."

Brenton R. Schlender," Small Advertising Agencies Often Resort to

Gimmicks to Grab Attention of Clients," *Wall Street Journal*, February 12, 1988, p. 15.

David E. Rosenbaum, "Congress Mulls a Commercial Break," *New York Times,* Section 4, February 22, 1998, p. 5. Can Congress prohibit tobacco companies from advertising? Or does the first amendment protect commercial speech as well? The article besides raising these questions reports on a study that found that 1/3 of teenagers aged 12- to 17-year olds were affected by tobacco ads and thus 2/3rds were not.

Elizabeth M. Whelan, "[Coke] Euro-Scare Isn't the 'Real Thing'," *Wall Street Journal,* June 21, 1999, p. A26. Reviews the Coke scare on the heels of the Dioxin scare in food supplies in Belgium.

Timothy Noah, "People's Choice Awards," *The New York Times Magazine,* August 8, 1999, pp. 42–45. Which is more reliable consumer polling data or expert reviews such as Consumer Reports magazine? The article focuses on the rise of J. D. Power & Associates with its polling data.

Tim Parks, *Adultery and Other Diversions* (New York: Arcade Publishing Company, 1999). For a discussion of how Benetton uses shock ads to garner publicity and how it seduces writers as well to provide the cover of social responsibility, see the chapter entitled "Charity" pp. 97–111.

4

The Game of Political Economy

> We cannot safely leave politics to politicians, or political economy to college professors.
>
> —Henry George

While *political economy* since Adam Smith's time suggests a unity of subject, the two have diverged and danced to different tunes. They are two different "games" with different rules and objectives. Moreover, whether in democracies or in totalitarian nations, the political system as an envelope and *driver* has the ultimate power to define, to redraw boundaries, and to subsume all private economic activity—in short the power to *abolish* the other game. Schematically let us examine the two games:

Two Games

Game	price system	representative government
Players	consumers	citizens
Ball	$$$$/wealth	power
Uniform	none(equity)	yes(equality)
Umpire	marketplace competition	ballot box, legislative arena and courts
Goals	material well being:	order, justice, freedom:

the production & the consumption of goods & services predicated on private property & competition	people may adopt a Jeffersonian role of limited government, or an intermediate stage of welfare and a regulatory states or to the complete adoption of a socialist society making the gov't a *super-monopolist* with no competition

As examples of cross-overs in the two games, consider the anti-trust suit launched in 1999 against Microsoft. It illustrates how competitors unable to defeat Microsoft in the marketplace sought political "solutions." Also, the steel industry similarly uses so-called anti-dumping trade rules to hobble foreign steel exporters. In both cases, the winners are few, the losers many in our economy.

While the patron saints of a market economy are Adam Smith and David Ricardo, the hovering angels of politics vary depending on the reach of government into daily life. As noted, Jefferson believed in a limited role for government restricted to the essentials of maintaining order while Hamilton and Lincoln took an expansive view that what the citizens could not do singly, the government could do collectively. Of the wish for a full-blown socialist society, the last formal apostle in America was Norman Thomas. After the collapse of the Soviet Union, only closet socialists remain, scattered in the media and foundations, but mostly in the universities.

Nevertheless our purposes are restricted to the guises of persuasion not a discourse on power and wealth. Thus we confine the following remarks to the political game as chapter two confined itself to the products of the marketplace. In politics there are three basic rules of the game: 1) to get elected; 2) to stay elected; and 3) "to get along in the game, go along." But surely this is too cynical a view of politics? No doubt by half.

We leave to philosophers and pundits the question of whether politics as played today is a necessary evil or a costly misadventure in discharging public purposes. Aside from other roles, the paramount role of politicians acting collectively is to avoid fiscal excess, that is, the propagation of the illusion that the whole of fiscal revenues are greater than the sum total of tax receipts. To indulge in this folly of endless budget deficits is to invite inflation and other unintended consequences. For politicians inflation in the past provided that ultimate sleight of hands filling the glass of prosperity with bubbles. While Congressional Republicans strove to balance the federal budget, President Clinton refused to cut expenditures and insisted that the budget could not be balanced before 2010 but he was skillful in taking credit when the economy of the 1990s generated new jobs and overflowing taxes into the U.S. Treasury. But for our purposes of adumbrating the art of persuasion, we simply recite the above facts, propositions and illusions of political life and move on.

In the preceding chapter, we noted that commercial messages were directed primarily to exchanges and to a lesser degree of imperative messages to cease certain personal and social behaviors. In this chapter we focus on messages directed by politicians to the electorate. Unfortunately, the tag of propaganda and spinning is often applied solely to politicians and government news handouts when in fact it encompasses as we have enumerated other agents of persuasion.

Today when advertising agencies run political campaigns it is no surprise that the trio of gimmicks, genres and devices used to sell products or to counter anti-social behavior are used to sell politicians. Whether selling products, people or ideas, the Madison Avenue fraternity stands ready to offer its services. But the political realm differs in at least one aspect from the selling of products: the unmentionable emotions including anger and fear that Hayakawa mentioned and today race-baiting.

For example, the anti-Barry Goldwater TV ad in the 1964 presidential election campaign comes to mind in which a nuclear countdown is superimposed on a child picking daisies. So powerful was the television version that it was withdrawn immediately by the National Democratic Committee over Republican cries of outrage. The printed version appears below.

The alarmist technique featured in a 1964 poster of The Women's Strike For Peace Information Clearinghouse. Similar material was used in television ads of the National Democratic Committee.

Political passions were aroused again nearly a quarter of a century later when the nomination of Judge Robert Bork to the US Supreme Court was defeated. A review of the episode constitutes an excellent primer on the uses of the politics of destruction and endless spinning. As one writer puts it, "In today's parlance, spin stands for fabrication. Spin doctors try to alter the facts through a deliberate and reckless disregard fro the truth." Lying by politicians becomes as easy as breathing.

At this juncture it is well to distinguish the twin lives of legislators. First the task of getting elected by mounting a campaign, delivering speeches, pressing the flesh, appearing in television ads, and raising campaign funds relies heavily on the skills of persuasion whether they draw on the talents of public relations firms, advertising agencies or spin doctors. The second involves the legislative work of politicians that includes serving on committees to elicit information in all its guises: studies, consultants, public testimony and finally the casting of votes. For the most part, legislators are responsible individuals with their share of greed, ambition and venality as the "Keating Five" scandal illustrated involving US Senators including John Glenn.

When Senator Joseph R. McCarthy in February of 1950 held aloft in his hand a sheet of paper with those magical words that began an era,

"I hold here in my hand a list of..." the witch-hunt for subversives had begun. In the process a new phrase entered the political lexicon: "McCarthyite tactics." These tactics included accusation, and once reported by the press, which for the accused began the long journey of guilt by headline, mud slinging, card stacking and guilt by association. The result was that jobs were lost, reputations destroyed while countless others lived under a spell of fear.

But McCarthy and his staff were adroit for at least four years in keeping the forces of fair play at bay. Finally in 1954, the US Senate censured McCarthy, and from this point, the press that had dutifully reported his inquisitorial antics on the front pages now relegated him to the back pages.

To begin our look at politics we must mention the obvious. The mother's milk of political campaigning is money. Secondly to speak to the already converted makes campaigning a bit easier. Thirdly, to reward the converted, the politician will choose either the left or right column of sparkling generalities to warm the cockles of the party faithful. Familiarity does not elicit contempt only the warm glow of the bandwagon.

A	B
affirmative action	equality of opportunity
entitlements	there is no free lunch
nuclear freeze	military strength
peace now	no unilateral disarmament
end poverty	create jobs and wealth
rights	responsibilities
equality of results	equality of opportunity
end global warming	more economic growth

Now let us join, by way of illustration, US Senator Bob Fudgebottom on the campaign trail. One night after dinner at a fundraiser in his honor, the Senator delivered a warm and sparkling speech to his admirers.

"My friends, it gives me great pleasure to address this august assembly this evening. It gives me pleasure as your Senator in Washington—what with all the major problems and issues facing the nation—well, the opportunity to get back home, to the grass roots, to you good people, makes my job all the more worthwhile. While the responsibilities of my office are great, I welcome the opportunity to serve the people of our great state, New Indiana. Needless to say, I am pleased that on this cold winter night all of you came out to break bread with Jean and me.

"Notwithstanding the negative campaign by my opponent, I believe the people of this great state will place their trust in me for another term in the Senate. My opponent alludes to the fact that I have been evasive in outlining my program. Well, I ask you, ladies and gentlemen, is there any reason to answer this silly point? All of you are quite aware what I stand for. Why a look at my record in the Senate will prove it.

"As you know, I have done my utmost to protect the environment, to see that our farmers get a fair shake, and that the "little people" have a voice in Congress. And I say this with all honesty and pride that no senator has been more pro-American in protecting jobs and in fostering a "buy American" attitude among our people. Nor have I been lulled by the siren calls of isolationism. No we can only remain strong and enjoy the blessings of liberty and the pursuit of happiness by maintaining a strong defense. Our steadfastness has brought us deliverance. First the Berlin Wall fell and then the Evil Empire. But there remain rogue nations from North Korea to Iraq with mischief on their minds.

"Now more than ever I believe and have always fought for the Jeffersonian ideal that the government which rules least, governs best. Of course there are exceptions. But we must not destroy the golden calf of free enterprise by over-regulation and high taxes. If not, our standard of living, our freedoms and our way of life may well be threatened. At a time of budget surpluses, we must shun new social programs no matter how desirable. We all know how these programs start modestly with a $100 million expenditure, but within five years the program will have grown to $10 billion and a few years later to $100 billion. In this regard, I am afraid that politics as usual, like business as usual, may well be dangerous to the well being of the nation.

"No, my friends, we can not get something for nothing. To look to Washington for the answer (or at least dollars) for every issue that comes along may well bankrupt us. The price would be too high. Therefore as our forebears understood only too well, and we must relearn, anew, it is only through hard work, thrift, community spirit, voluntary action and a belief in the Almighty that will carry this great nation forward to her destiny."

The following night, Senator Fudgebottom and his wife were in attendance at the *Do Good Society* when Ignatius Stringfellow, the president delivered a few remarks to the faithful:

"Now, more than ever, we must stand firm for what we believe and hold dear. It will not be easy. To stand firm in our convictions is to invite abuse and ridicule from our opponents as 'dewy-eyed idealists,' "knee-jerk liberalism" and worse. But we can stand the heat. Nor should we be concerned solely with our comfort at this moment of crisis in our nation's history. We must not count the personal cost, but keep our vision clear, and strive for a future that will vindicate our efforts.

"We must stand together, or as the adage indicates, we will suffer individually by failing to achieve our common ends. Of course some of us have minor reservations about this or that, but there is no division, no disagreement, no quibbling over substance. As to the central core of shared beliefs we are one.

"Since we are being tested, we shall respond. To do less is to cheat our posterity and deny us the kind of world we want our children to live in. Thus we must strive and protest again, demonstrate and march again, write and demand again until we are triumphant. Fairness. Equality. Population control. End capital punishment. End global warming. End gene experiments. End the twentieth century! On these building blocks we shall be heard. Tonight Senator Fudgebottom joins us in wishing our cause well. A salute to the Senator!

"So tonight let us renew our arduous journey on the road to national revival. Until recent times, our cause has had no focus, no institutional voice. But armed with your donations and our friends in the media, our attorneys have been skillful in blocking our foes by using the fine points of the law to our advantage. As to unwanted laws, we can delay and stall until hell freezes over. As to the courts, such is the beauty of the 'due process' clause in the Bill of Rights that it offers as far as the eye can see endless appeals. So any attacks on our cause whether real or imagined, we have repelled. But withal we must remain humble in our pride that our cause is just and right. To this ideal of goodness and compassion, we pledge ourselves. Join us in our crusade." [Pledge cards and envelopes were available in the rear of the ballroom.]

*

Aside from countless glittering generalities, politicians and do-gooders love to surround themselves with suitable symbols. A typical ad will show the politician seated with the flag to one side, law books behind, and photographs of the family prominently displayed: all revealing the touchstones of patriotism, learning, and family. Related to the symbols are the ability to coin slogans such as the Square Deal, the New Deal and the Great Society. Some slogans resonate for a time then evaporate. Without substance, slogans are merely the equivalent of gimmicks in commercial ads that seek to grab the attention of the busy consumer and citizen. Whether the goals of modern persuasion are conducive to the interests of the good citizen and the public interest are questions deferred to chapter seven.

Thus far we have ignored time, but it is never far from the minds of those engaged in persuasion. When Vance Packard in *The Hidden Persuaders* sounded the alarm about subliminal persuasion in the 1950, it was seen as a curiosity. Today the rock culture and MTV give us the strobe lights, quick cuts, loud music and sex moving willing customers well below the threshold of persuasion. No doubt Packard would feel vindicated. So busy and bored people must be grabbed more often by their desires lest they fail to allot twenty seconds to the message. Now, we live with the *ten second* commercial. Imagine how that focuses the mind of the producer of the ads. Hence political and commercial slogans are the currency of our times: "Join the Pepsi generation;" "We will sell no wine before its time;" "you only go around once;" "when you care to send the very best;" and once upon a time, "Remember Pearl Harbor".

Before we leave formal politics, it is fitting to observe that throughout our history we have had both political and religious speakers who have demonstrated powers of persuasion and flamboyance. There is often a thin line between flamboyance of gesture and cadence and the fires of a demagogue playing on fears and prejudices of the audience. William Jennings Bryan illustrates the former while Huey Long, Theodore Bilbo, Tom Watson and Joe McCarthy illustrates the latter.

Before radio and television, politicians were expected to entertain and to deliver orotund homilies not unlike our Senator Fudgebottom. But today, much as the stage actor must unlearn certain skills in order to perform before the smaller frame of television, so politicians have had to develop other skills not the least of having photogenic appeal. Akin to Gresham's law, in the currency of politics the stress on appearance drives out other qualities.

This had led one historian to surmise that many of our former presidents would have done poorly on television. Both Washington and Lincoln would have spoken slowly with the cardinal sin of dead air time between question and answer. Nor as another historian noted was Jefferson ever "an effective public speaker." To all the other infirmities of running for political office, the television barrier may be the most forbidding or enticing.

Marya Mannes long ago gave us the lay of the political land as follows:

> "The experts instructed the politicians…in the techniques of dressing, talking, gesturing, and looking sincere…"
>
> —*New York Times*

Look the camera in the eye,
Keep the chin line firm,
Sit with nonchalance and try
Not to shift or squirm.

When you speak of origins,
Family, or life,
Cultivate the boyish grin
That won your girlish wife.

Let the mouth be grim and straight
When you talk of prayer,
Morality, the Soviet State,
And Freedom Everywhere.

Never rise above your kind
Even if you could:
To have an ordinary mind
Is for the common good.

All this know you should know by now,
The model has been clear:
It's never what you say, but how
You make it sound sincere.

Playing the game of sincerity is hard work for politicians. To assist them, the birth of "spin doctors" came of age in the 1980s and to fruition with the presidency of Bill Clinton. One cardinal technique of spinning is to open with a lie and then proceed in the next breath with a further lie. Or as a variant one can start a speech, a campaign, a TV-ad with a partial truth and segue into lies. As Christopher Matthews has written reporters and readers rarely if ever get beyond the first spin. Thus would-be demagogues can thrive in a democratic culture.

Free Time Activities

IDENTIFY the various techniques of persuasion in the Fudgebottom and Stringfellow speeches.

SEE: Senator Joseph McCarthy in action by renting the videocassette of the 1954 McCarthy/US Army hearings.

READ for further information and pleasure:

a) On Huey Long's life read the novel based on his life by Robert Penn Warren, *All the King's Men*. See also the movie of the same name.

b) On Senator Joe McCarthy, *read* William Buckley, *McCarthy and His Enemies* (1954); and Richard Rovere, *Senator Joe McCarthy* (1959), the former writer a defender, the latter a critic of the late senator's public career. For new perspectives by historians on McCarthy, *read* Ethan Bronner, "Rethinking McCarthyism, if Not McCarthy," *New York Times,* October 18, 1998, Section 4, pp. 1, 6. *Read* also, Allen Weinstein & Alexander Vassiliev, *The Haunted Wood* (1998), on the actual numbers of Americans spying for the Soviet Union during the 1930s and 1940s. For a recent reassessment, see Arthur Herman, *Joseph McCarthy: Reexamining the Life and Legacy of America's Most Hated Senator* (2000).

c) On sundry demagogues, *read* A. Michie & R. Rylick, *Dixie Demagogues* (1939).

d) On Tom Watson, *read* Hodding Carter, *The Angry Scar* (1959) and C. Vann Woodward, *Agrarian Rebel: Tom Watson* (1955). Watson began as an agrarian rebel but turned into a demagogue; he made a cameo appearance in the Leo Frank/Mary Phagan murder trial in Georgia. In early 1988, NBC-TV presented a dramatization of the case.

e) On the art of lying *read* Sissela Bok, *Lying* (1979) and David Wise, *The Politics of Lying* (1973). Both authors offer numerous examples of *deception* as the daily lifeblood of politicians.

f) On Robert Bork, *read* Suzanne Garment, "The War Against Robert H. Bork," *Commentary*, January 1988, pp. 17–26; L. Gordon Crovitz, "The Frankensteining of Bork," *Wall Street Journal*, October 14, 1987, p. 32; William Safire, "Judge Bork's Victory," *New York Times*, October 11, 1987, Section 4, p. 27.

g) Television commercials are difficult to locate. But the political ads of 1994 and 1995 by both the Republicans opposed to the Clinton health plan, and the Democratic National Committee ads denouncing Republican "cuts" in school lunches, Medicare, etc. are worth reviewing. More fundamentally, can ads be countered by facts, principles and logic? Or must emotional ads be fought with emotional ads? Lies with lies? What are the implications for society, and for government of this path toward Orwellian doublethink?

h) On spinning, *read* Christopher Matthews, "Doesn't He [Clinton] Ever Get Dizzy?" *Wall Street Journal,* August 5, 1998, p. A14.

i) *See* Bill Moyers, "Free Speech on Sale," *PBS-TV*, June 8, 1999. After reviewing the tape consider 1) the lack of historical context, 2) the lack of political context in how politicians extract campaign funds [see Fred McChesney, *Money for Nothing* (1997); the lack of balance in how government curtails freedom of speech, and property rights (see James Bovard's *Freedom in Chains* (1999) and Richard Pipes' *Property and Freedom* (1999)].

Political Economy Notes

Books

James T. Bennett & Thomas J. DiLorenzo, *Official Lies: How Washington Misleads Us* (Alexandra, VA: Groom Books, 1992).

Michael C. Choukas, *Propaganda Comes of Age, op. cit.*, p. 209, for the anti-Goldwater ad and caption.

Tyrell R. Emmett, *Boy Clinton: the Political Biography* (Washington, D.C.: Regnery Pub., 1996).

Paul Greenburg, *No Surprises: Two Decades of Clinton-Watching* (Washington, D.C.: Brassey's, 1996).

Tom Graham, *Pattern of Deception: the Media's Role in the Clinton Presidency* (Alexandria, VA: Media Research Center, 1996).

Howard Kurtz, *Spin Cycle: Inside the Clinton Propaganda Machine* (New York: Free Press, 1998).

Richard A. Posner, *An Affair of State* (Cambridge: Harvard University Press, 1999). A careful review of President Clinton's impeachment case.

Richard Reeves, *Running in Place: How Bill Clinton Disappointed America* (Kansas City, MO: Andrews and McNeel, 1996).

Ed Rollins, *Bare Knuckles and Back Rooms* (New York: Broadway Books, 1996). See pp. 363–364 for "Rollins's Rules of Campaign Combat."

James B. Stewart, *Blood Sport: The President and His Adversaries* (New York: Simon & Schuster, 1996).

Deborah J. Stone & Christopher Manion, *"Slick Willie" II: Why America Still Cannot Trust Bill Clinton* (Annapolis, MD: Annapolis-Washington Book Pub., 1994).

Kevin H. Watson, *The Clinton Record: Everything Bill and Hillary Want You to Forget* (Bellevue, WA: Merrill Press, 1996).

Periodicals

Henry S. Commager, "Washington Would Have Lost a TV Debate," *New York Times Magazine*, October 30, 1960, p. 13ff.

Robert L. Dilenschneider, "'Spin Doctors' Practice Public Relations Quackery," *Wall Street Journal,* June 1, 1998, p. A18. "In today's parlance, spin stands for fabrication. Spin doctors try to alter the facts through a deliberate and reckless disregard for the truth."

Henry Fairlie, "An Englishman Goes to a Klan Meeting," *New York Times Magazine*, May 23, 1965, p. 26ff. Fairlie attended a KKK meeting which included an attempt to burn a cross. But he concluded, "How the camera can lie! There was nothing as melodramatic or as eerie in this ritual as the color photographs, carefully trimmed for effect, suggest...But the old rugged cross would not burn." P.84.

Jeff Gerth, "Clinton's Top Fund-Raiser Made Pile for Himself," *New York Times,* December 12, 1999, NE, pp. 1, 38. Through the alchemy of politics, power turns into money, millions of dollars for Clinton and millions for his fundraiser.

Paul A. Gigot, "What Nixon Taught Dems About Race," *Wall Street Journal*, October 29, 1999, p. A18. The use of election eve bombshells particularly "race-baiting."

Albert R. Hunt, "'The Show Horse' Rep. Pressler Works Hard to Create Image, Not to Create Laws," *Wall Street Journal*, May 20, 1977, pp. 1, 31.

Thomas Keiser, " 'The Illinois Beast': One of Our Greatest Presidents," *Wall Street Journal*, February 11, 1988, p. 22, recounts some of the unflattering comments that Lincoln was subjected to by his contemporaries such as: "gorilla," "political coward," "filthy story teller," "half-witted usurper," "obscene clown," and "unmentionably diseased."

Richard Klein, "The Tobacco Deal: Prohibition II," *Wall Street Journal*, June 26, 1997, p. A18. Elizabeth M Whelan, "The Tobacco Deal: Or a Purveyor of Poison?" *Wall Street Journal*, June 26, 1997, p. A18.

Elizabeth Kolbert, "In [Political] Campaign Ads, Only the Names Have Changed," *New York Times*, January 14, 1996, Section 4, p. 5.

Charles Krauthammer, "President's Seattle [WTO] Stunt Completely in Character," *Seattle Times*, December 13, 1999, p. B4. Clinton both derailed the WTO talks and gave aid and comfort to the street protesters.

Kerry Lauerman, "Block the Vote," *New York Times Magazine*, January 23, 2000, p. 16. A review of negative ads with illustrations, and the notion that not advertising a candidate may lead to a desirable low voter turnout.

John Leo, "The Dirty Little Secrets Employed by the Pollsters," *Seattle Times,* October 12, 1999, p. B5. Leo contends that most polls are card-stacked, rigged to produce a given conclusion and that politicians and the press increasingly rely on them as "news" rather than as pieces of persuasion.

Lexington, "The [Political] Rules of the Game," *The Economist,* November 2, 1996, p. 30. Ten pertinent rules.

Michelle Malkin, "The Bizarre Tobacco Deal Is a Threat to Our Liberty," *Seattle Times*, June 24, 1997, p. B4.

Christopher Matthews," Tip O'Neill's Tips for the GOP," *Wall Street Journal,* October 29, 1999, p. A18. Matthews offer four rules but illustrates Clinton's demagoguery on welfare reform and balancing the budget.

Martha T. Moore, "Political Ads: The Camera Can Tell Lies," *USA Today*, May 23, 1996, p. 6A.

Peggy Noonan, "The Mad Boomer [Hillary Clinton]," *Wall Street Journal,* June 8, 1999, p. A18. Machiavellian politics on display as politicians used "words and images not to reveal but to obscure, not to clarify but to confuse. They would mislead their way to power."

Arthur M. Schlesinger Jr., "The Ultimate Approval Rating [of Presidents]," *New York Times Magazine*, December 15, 1996, pp. 46–51.

Gerald F. Seib, "Heard Enough Negative Ads? [Senator Chuck] Hagel Has, Too," *Wall Street Journal,* November 25, 1998, p. A20.

Michael Wines, "Supreme Leader, Pigeon in Chief," *New York Times*, March 23, 1997, Section 4, pp. 1, 5. A brief history of name-calling of our presidents from Washington to Clinton.

Geoffrey Wheatcroft, "'McCarthyism' Is Becoming Orwellian," *Wall Street Journal*, February 9, 2000, p. A26. The author reviews the misuse and overuse today of both terms: McCarthyism and Orwellian.

5

Street Games

Everyday we protest, therefore we exist.

—Anon

Do street protests persuade? Like any advertisement, it depends on whether the protesters proffer a specific remedy or solution. Or like institutional ads, the protesters seek the glow of psychological or symbolic affirmation. Over the course of our history, the repertoire of street persuasions for Americans have involved spontaneous and organized group activities in the form of marches, parades, petitions and picketing usually of government agencies, at other times of business firms. More recently we have protests, marches and violence directed toward international agencies such as the 1999 World Trade Organization meeting in Seattle.

By the late nineteenth century it was clear that group activity had supplanted solitary endeavors of voting, writing letters to the editor or to his senator, or by running for political office. For much of the nineteenth century marches and protests sought specific remedies on specific subjects such as the abolition of slavery, the securing of women's suffrage, the prohibition of alcohol by the temperance movement and later attempts at organizing labor.

By mid-twentieth century, the civil rights movement led by Martin Luther King accomplished much and saw fruition by the mid 1960s with the passage of civil rights acts. No sooner had federal legislation passed than King's voice was supplanted by the strident rhetoric of Eldridge Cleaver, Huey Newton, Bobby Seale, Malcolm X and Stokely Carmichael. The civil rights movement gave way to black power and black separatism with the symbols of clenched fists, rifles, black leather, black shades and menace on the wing. Symbolism and psychological separatism were also the order of the day.

The decade of the sixties was the hothouse that saw an explosion in both the number and scale of demonstrations and protests. The Vietnam War unleashed anti-war and anti-draft protests in the form of demonstrations, sit-ins, draft-card burnings and flight by draft-evaders to Canada and Sweden. Another segment of bored youth unwilling to enter the labor force or study in school turned to guerrilla theater on university campuses. Leveraging their "idealism", they asserted their instant knowledge of how institutions functioned, how knowledge was gained, how cultures were transmitted, and how societies and economies worked, and above all, proceeded to lecture their betters including their parents on personal and societal failures. To the true believers in the virtues of the young, these temper tantrums were but symbolic affirmations of idealism. What wrongs had been remedied?

And then there were the riots beginning with Watts in 1965, followed subsequently in Newark and Detroit, Washington and other cities. It became fashionable among pundits and journalists in the 1960s to insist that the riots were a permanent feature of American life, that is, long, hot summers every year for the foreseeable future. Of course, it was not true, even righteous rage wears out. Destroying neighborhoods and businesses is subject to diminishing returns as more and more stores are firebombed and depleted. Close to forty years later, many of these war-torn neighborhoods have yet to recover from what some thought as justifiable means of redress. Of what wrongs by whom? Of what psychological good?

Yet these inner-city street rioters and college student rumblings could have taken place on different planets for all their similarities. For these collegiate truants from studies were soon joined by their vagabond counterparts in search of endless adolescence. The new Mecca was Haight-Ashbury with satellites in Greenwich Village, Amsterdam and Berlin. Domestically, the adherents of the counterculture dismissed work, marriage, study, and military service all the while insisting on endless pursuit of pleasure, release from any social constraint and the awaiting, at least for Americans, of the greening of America.

The Age of Aquarius had arrived sans thought except to give birth to the free lunch society. While a majority in society continued to work, pay taxes, raise families and serve in the military, in short, "minding the store" of society, the truants took acid trips, engaged in unlimited sex, and expressed themselves in grunts and four letter words. To garb themselves they turned to Depression rags that their grandparents had worn of necessity. With their new uniforms and poses, they blew their minds with drugs and decibel shattering rock. So as the decade ended the resulting stance was one of rebellion against the draft, against the Pentagon, against Lyndon Johnson, against the work ethic and the family, and against authority.

But these juvenile pranks by footloose and free middle class youngsters could not have been validated without the abdication of many adults of their responsibility to shout and call-out that the idealists were culturally naked. Adult wisdom based on hard-won experience, knowledge, culture, religion, and common sense was dismissed lest they appear to their children of privilege as nay-sayers. Saying no to know-nothings became politically incorrect. And so by turns, many parents, college professors and administrators, journalists and politicians not to mention judges gave tacit approval to these truants thumbing their noses at the civil society. And at their parents.

But parents in denial could watch their off-springs on the nightly TV news frolicking away during the sixties in demonstrations, sit-ins at Columbia University, chain-ins at federal buildings and on bridges, marches to the Pentagon, and Woodstock.

On another front, Mau-mauing became a tool to intimidate local officials by menace and guilt-mongering so as to ostensibly obtain public jobs, the turning over of vacant public buildings to community activists and finally handing out "walking around money" for these protesters. Many mayors acquiesced in these bribes in the name of justice and compassion.

Another side to these free-form demonstrations was the blurring of public and private realms. Once upon a time, all Americans respected the distinction between public and private matters, between public forums and private residences. In the late twentieth century these demarcations vanished along with much else of civility.

And so in time, protests went from public forums to private homes. It began in Chicago with the picketing of the home of Mayor Richard Daley. A decade later in Seattle, those opposed to apartheid picketed the residence of the South African consul. By the 1980s and later, the homes of physicians performing abortions were subject to picketing, harassing phone calls, hate mail and death threats. In Florida a physician practicing abortion was murdered. Similarly AIDS' activists followed suit in harassing physicians at their homes who did not toe the AIDS party line.

But it was the 1968 Democratic Convention that remains vivid in the public's recollection thanks to the distortions of the television networks. Anti-war activists carefully planned their guerrilla tactics to incite the Chicago police and succeeded beyond their wildest imaginings. The TV cameras did *not* record the planning, and the provocations only the police seemingly out of control.

And then they had that wonderful footage of an angry mayor, Richard Daley, who had been deliberately boxed-in and ill-used by the activists. To add insult to injury of Daley, fellow Democrats within the convention denounced the Chicago police while pearly voiced TV anchors gleefully showed the police in front of the delegates' hotels weighing into the crowd of protesters. Daley and Chicago's civic reputation lay in tatters.

Not surprisingly, every ten years of so, the TV networks dust off their film footage of the 1960s, especially 1968, and add a new a voice over but with no attempt to find out what truly happened. It would be politically incorrect. Instead Chicago and Mayor Daley were cast as the "bad guys" while the "student" protestors were cast as the "good guys." Thus, we await patiently a careful history of the 1960s including the fateful year of 1968. All in all the sixties gave us the trio of street violence, street theater and media circuses. More on this latter point in chapter nine.

But there is a free-lance activity, sometimes done in concert with others that lingers today and throughout the world. Graffiti is the ultimate street game of our age. Apologists are quick to dismiss graffiti as a juvenile assertion of self-esteem or to praise the desecrations as street works of art. But such double-speak ignores graffiti's sustained attack upon the sense of order and community well being. Graffiti sprayers seek neither civic virtue nor honest work but confirmation in the brotherhood of vandals. Public vandalism, no; private graffiti of one's body by piercing and tattooing, of course.

Finally, do street games persuade? In the 1960s some did, many did not. Not persuasion but protest for protest's sake became for many the only point. For example, the Provos of Holland in the 1960s illustrated this romantic stance riding their white bicycles of protest while handing out blank sheets of paper. The fun was in the exhibition.

Today environmental "greens" engage in various demonstrations in one direction: *stop everything*. The messages and slogans are: stop the hunting of whales; stop global warming; stop population growth; stop genetic modified foods; stop animal testing; stop logging of old redwood trees; stop tobacco use and withdraw to an Arcadia that never was.

Free timeActivities

IDENTIFY how many street protests and demonstrations took place in your community during the last year. On what issues?

IDENTIFY the volume and degree of graffiti in your community. Do the police take graffiti seriously? If not, what civic actions have been taken to counter public vandalism?

JOIN a protest march and chat with the protesters as to how many protests of late they have been involved. To the protesters does it matter if they "succeed" in their marches and demonstrations? Or is the marching self-sufficient and satisfying as street theater?

Street Games Notes

Books

Edward C. Banfield, *The Unheavenly City* (Boston: Little, Brown & Co., 1970). See especially Chapter nine, "Rioting Mainly for Fun and Profit."

Myron Magnet, *The Dream and the Nightmare: the Sixties' Legacy to the Underclass* (New York: William Morrow & Co., 1993). Magnet reviews the discrepancy between good intentions and dire social consequences.

Charles Perry, *Haight-Ashbury: A History* (New York: Random House, 1985).

Periodicals

Cynthia Crossen, "Shock Troops: AIDS Activists," *Wall Street Journal*, December 7, 1989, p. A.

Daniel Harris, "Making Kitsch from AIDS," *Harper's*, July 1994, pp. 55–60.

Eugene Kennedy, "The Year [1968] That Shook Chicago," *New York Times Magazine*, March 5, 1978, p. 27ff.

Irving Kristol, "AIDS and False Innocence," *Wall Street Journal*, August 6, 1992, p. A14.

Joseph Lelyveld, "Dadaists [Provos] in Politics," *New York Times Magazine*, October 2, 1966, p. 32ff.

Jane & Michael Stern, "Decent Exposure," *The New Yorker*, March 19, 1990, p. 76. As one free-lance activist stated at a pro-nudist demonstration, "*Today, we protested all morning with the pro-choice people...Last week we were at the Oak Hill Country Club with the Anti-Apartheid Coalition. Next, we're going to a march with the gay community...*" (italics added).

*

Appendix A: WTO Meeting in Seattle

For articles on the World Trade Organization [WTO] meeting in Seattle, November 29 through December 3, 1999 and other coverage, see the following:

First, did the press and TV news seek to provide a *context* for the daily events as follows?

1) Did reporters seek answers to basic questions? Of the protesters: Who were they? Where did they come from? Who paid their fare to Seattle? What group(s) were they members of? Were these people unemployed or what? Since, judging from photos and TV coverage, a number of the protesters were young of high school or college age, who recruited them?

2) Did any of the press or TV reporters seek to compile each day a directory of all the groups (with their phone numbers listed and addresses) taking part in the "protests"?

3) As to the notion that the first amendment permits preventing people from entering a public building, or a mob of protesters chaining themselves to the doors of the Westin Hotel, did the press and TV news provide some legal background on this? When and where does freedom of assembly for some mean that other Americans have to give up their rights to freely move about? Has the US Supreme Court blessed this behavior and when? As for the local newspaper, did the *Seattle Times* use or call upon the faculty at the University of Washington law school? Did the national newspapers similarly call upon legal experts for information?

4) Did the press and TV news seek to explain what free trade is all about? Rather than an abstruse depiction of relative and absolute advantage, did they present a catalog in table form of our exports on one side and our imports on the other. Surely this information was fundamental.

5) Was this rag-tag collection of "protesters" the last hurrah of socialists and communists plus the usual suspects of job protection via the longshoremen, machinists, steelworkers, etc.? And did President Clinton demagogue the issue so thoroughly that the WTO in the future would have to come up with a supposedly, human face. The "protesters" objected to what the WTO had done in the past as imperialism and then in the same breath insisted on new labor and environmental rules being foisted on the poorest nations! Was this trade policy akin to junk science, global warning and GMO sweeping Europe? Did we witness the new Luddites and "Know-nothings" of the new millennium?

Susan Nielsen, "WTO: 50,000 Rabbits and Not a Fact in Sight," *Seattle Times,* November 11, 1999, p. B6. SN outlined some bare facts as to what the WTO can and cannot do, that it is not evil, but "reflects the best and worst of its participant countries…" Destroy the environment? "Not true." She denounces the Roosevelt High School newspaper's editorial as silly when it asserts that the WTO shreds the US Constitution. She sharply criticized the Luddites and know-nothings along with the AFL-CIO which is in the job protection stance aka "fair trade".

C. Leigh Anderson, "WTO Can Move Debate on Trade, Environment to Middle Ground," *Seattle Post-Intelligencer,* November 21, 1999, pp. F1, F3. She is an associate professor in the school of public affairs at the UW. Generally this is a carefully analyzed article on the benefits of free trade. She stresses that free trade is beneficial especially for poorer countries. By raising their incomes it permits poorer nations the opportunity to tackle environmental and social improvements.

The one key omission in the article is the role of labor in protecting jobs; and the omission of the principle of comparative advantage, both relative and absolute.

Lisa Pemberton-Butler, "WTO Issues Unite Students: Teachers Stir Up Interest in Upcoming Trade Talks," *Seattle Times,* November 22, 1999, pp. B1, B2. A Renton High School teacher invited his students to take an interest in the WTO conference in Seattle, and then invited the "protesters" to visit his classroom and spread their point of view, to wit, that free trade thrives on sweatshop conditions overseas. The protesters urged students to be truant on November 30th and protest! The article also noted that student protestors from the UW and Seattle high school would participate! The Renton HS teacher, Dutch Day, said he wanted a different viewpoint to counteract the media's pro WTO stance. Hence there were no speakers for free trade.

Joshua Robin, "Keeping the Peace Among [WTO] Protesters," *Seattle Times,* November 22, 1999, pp. B1, B2. Students and AFL-CIO are training peace-monitors and marshals to keep the demonstrations orderly.

David Postman, et. al, "Confusion Grips WTO Warm-Up," *Seattle Times,* November 29, 1999, pp. A1, A14.

David Postman, " Right Meets Left in Protest, But for Different Reasons," *Seattle Times,* November 29, 1999, p. A12.

Stephen Dunphy, "Unions Press WTO for Labor Rights," *Seattle Times,* November 29, 1999, p. A13.

David Postman, et. al, "Tear Gas in Streets of Seattle," *Seattle Times,* November 30, 1999, pp. A1, A21

Stephen Dunphy, "[Ministers] Numbers Low for Besieged WTO Opening," *Seattle Times,* November 30, 1999, pp. A1, A22.

Mike Carter, "KOMO-TV Announces It Won't Cover 'Irresponsible or Illegal' Activities," *Seattle Times,* November 30, 1999, p. A23. But the KOMO news director's statement that the station was "taking a stand on not giving some protest groups the publicity they want." This drew a retort from Ben Bagdikian, retired dean of journalism at the U of California Berkeley that the disruptive and illegal protests were "all the more worthy of coverage" both as a public service and to give a voice to the disenfranchised in America!

Helene Cooper, "Some Hazy, Some Erudite and All Angry: Diversity of WTO Protests Makes Them Hard to Dismiss," *Wall Street Journal,* November 30, 1999, pp. A2, A12.

George Melloan, "Welcome to the Seattle World's Fair, Circa 1999," *Wall Street Journal,* November 30, 1999, p. A27. "The transition to a world in which 'globalization' makes some jobs less secure, even while it is making the overall economy wealthier, will be more traumatic in Europe than in the U.S., simply because there are more unionized workers enjoying state protections in Europe."
"In Seattle, the demonstrators will demand that the clock be turned back to a simpler age. But that is not going to happen. The folks who can't stand prosperity will ultimately have to yield to those who employ their talents and energies to creating it. It has always been that way."

Jack Broom, et. al, "Protesters Banned, Arrested," *Seattle Times,* December 1, 1999, pp. A1, A12.

David Postman & Mike Carter, "Police Switch to New Strategy," *Seattle Times,* December 1, 1999, pp. A1, A14.

David Postman, "Black-Clad Anarchists Target Cars, Windows and Reject Other's Pleas of 'No Violence'," *Seattle Times,* December 1, 1999, p. A12.

Kay Mcfadden, "[Local] TV Showed It Made a Difference," *Seattle Times,* December 1, 1999, p. A16. KM lauded KING-TV for its length of coverage and "strength in explanatory reporting and [that] provided a steady stream of context throughout the mayhem."

Helene Cooper, "Waves of Protest Disrupt WTO Meeting," *Wall Street Journal,* December 1, 1999, pp. A2, A12.

Francis Fukuyama, "The Left Should Love Globalization," *Wall Street Journal,* December 1, 1999, p. A26. "For the left, American imperialism has evolved into a new enemy, whose name is *globalization*." (Italics in original.) FF alludes to the fact that foreign workers allegedly working in sweatshop conditions have no alternatives if these jobs are shut down. [In fact many will drift back into grinding poverty and prostitution.] FF believes that the WTO in time will address labor and environmental concerns while governments provide retraining and other subsidies to those laid off.

Susan Nielsen, "Meaning of [WTO] Protests Blurs in Photo-Op of Century," *Seattle Times,* December 2, 1999, p. B4. She notes that video camcorders and camera were everywhere including the media. "What made the protests real? Mere experience seemed insufficient. Realness now requires the accumulation of proof." Become the media! "That's the positive spin. On the flip side, it's hard for a crowd not to wallow in self-awareness when it reflexively views itself through the lens of a TV camera."

Robert T. Nelson, et. al, "Shoppers Barred in Retail Core," *Seattle Times,* December 2, 1999, pp. A1, A24.

Tyrone Beason, "WTO Asked to Enforce Child Labor Ban," *Seattle Times,* December 2, 1999, p. A26. Several labor groups called on the WTO to ban child labor and insisted they were not asking for much except a minimum wage in all countries, the right of workers to bargain collectively and safe workplaces.

Patrick Harrington, "Steelworkers Rally Against WTO, 'Dumping,'" *Seattle Times,* December 2, 1999, p. A23. The steelworkers protested against cheap imports from Asia and the admission of China to the WTO.

Robert Guy Matthews, "U.S. Steel Industry Itself Gets Billions in Public Subsidies, Study Concludes," *Wall Street Journal,* November 29, 1999, p. B16. A study by the American Institute for International Steel reveals heavy federal and state subsidies for U.S. steel makers. The domestic steel companies challenge the study and insist that foreign steel companies receive massive domestic subsidies.

Helene Cooper, "Poorer Countries Are Demonstrators' Strongest Critics," *Wall Street Journal,* December 2, 1999, pp. A2, A8. What the protestors and organized labor wanted was the opposite of what poorer countries sought.

Editorial, "While the WTO Burns," *Wall Street Journal,* December 2, 1999, p. A22.

Thomas J. Deusterberg, "Free Trade Can Progress Without WTO," *Wall Street Journal,* December 2, 1999, p. A22. Free trade can be achieved from the bottom up through regional accords.

Geral F. Seib et. al, "Protests: Face of Future or Just a Blast From the Past?" *Wall Street Journal,* December 2, 1999, p. A8.

Rachel Zimmerman, "[Seattle] Police Stumble Despite Months of Preparation," *Wall Street Journal,* December 2, 1999, p. A8.

Bob Davis & Helene Cooper, "U.S. Worries About Future Trade Talks," *Wall Street Journal,* December 3, 1999, pp. A2, A8.

David Postman et. al, "Peace Settles Over Downtown," *Seattle Times,* December 3, 1999, pp. A1, A26.

Jim Brunner & Jack Broom, "Anarchists: They Play by Different Rules," *Seattle Times,* December 3, 1999, p. A25.

Associated Press, "Anarchists' Guru Says He's Proud," *Seattle Times,* December 3, 1999, p. A25.

Steve Miletich, "Police Weary After a Long Week," *Seattle Times,* December 3, 1999, p. A22. A photo accompanied this story showing two parents dressed in mock police gear with their nine year old daughter standing between them holding a placard "Citizens Against Police Agression"(sic).

Ian Ith & Janet Burkett, "Rally Protests Police Actions," *Seattle Times,* December 3, 1999, p. A22. The police on the night of December 1, directed protestors away from downtown to the Capitol Hill neighborhood and used tear gas and stun grenades to disperse crowds with the result that people in the neighborhood received the spill over of the noise and gas.

Kay McFadden, "KIRO-TV Keeps Eye on Police," *Seattle Times,* December 3, 1999, p. A25.

Anon., "[WTO] Conference Ends, Protests Don't," *Seattle Times,* December 4, 1999, p. A7. Street protestors demanding the release of jailed protestors surrounded the King County jail. Other protestors chained themselves to the doors of the Westin Hotel.

Stephen Dunphy, "WTO Group Will Leave Seattle With No Accord," *Seattle Times,* December 4, 1999, pp. A1, A5.

Steve Miletich & Nancy Bartley, "3 Charged With Felonies From Protest on Tuesday," *Seattle Times,* December 4, 1999, p. A7.

Anon., "Clueless In Seattle," *The Economist,* December 4, 1999, p. 17. "It is hard to say which was worse—watching the militant dunces parade their ignorance through the streets of Seattle, or listening to their lame-brained governments respond to the 'arguments.'"

Anon., "The New Trade War," *The Economist,* December 4, 1999, pp. 25–26.

Anon., "Countdown to Ruckus [in Seattle]," *The Economist,* December 4, 1999, p. 26. A look at the "...Ruckus Society and assorted other fringe groups..." demonstrating against the WTO meeting in Seattle.

Anon., "Who Needs the WTO?" *The Economist,* December 4, 1999, p. 74. "For anybody who supports liberal trade, the mere possibility that the WTO might now become a cause of economic retardation is deeply disturbing."

Timothy Egan, "New World Disorder: Free Trade Takes on Free Speech," *New York Times,* December 5, 1999, Section 4, pp. 1,5.

Joseph Kahn & David E. Sanger," Seattle Talks on Trade End With Stinging Blow to U.S." *New York Times,* December 5, 1999, NE, pp. 1, 14,

David E. Sanger, "The [WTO] Shipwreck in Seattle," *New York Times,* December 5, 1999, NE, p. 14. Why was the WTO meeting held? "...because Mr. Clinton was convinced that he had one last free-trade victory left."

Byron Acohido, "Deal Struck to Free All Jailed Protesters on Own Recognizance," *Seattle Times,* December 5, 1999, pp. A1, A16.

Chris Solomon, "[Anarchist] Squatters Vacate Downtown Building After 'Deal'," *Seattle Times,* December 5, 1999, p. A17. The deal involved the partial expropriation of private property in favor of units of the building to be put aside for the "homeless."

Anon., Letters to the Editors of the *Times, Seattle Times,* December 5, 1999, pp. B7-B8. Two pages of letters mostly from local residents but with a sprinkling of letters from across the nation. Interspersed on the two pages were two political cartoons and two photos. One of the photos had a caption showing an individual who had thrown a garbage can into a Starbucks' store window and then was photographed entering the store through the window. The initial portion of the caption was entitled "A WTO protester..." Even the editors of the Times had adopted the lexicon of the anarchists that the destruction of private property was legitimate "protest."

Bernard Wysocki Jr., "The WTO: the Villain in a Drama It Wrote," *Wall Street Journal,* December 6, 1999, p. A1.

Helene Cooper et. al, "WTO's Failure Bid to Launch Trade Talks Emboldens Protesters," *Wall Street Journal,* December 6, 1999, pp. A1, A17.

Peter Waldman, "An Anarchist Looks to Provide Logic to Coterie at Core of WTO Vandalism," *Wall Street Journal,* December 6, 1999, p. A17. An interview with John Zerzan, the guru of the anarchists who struck in Seattle, perhaps himself included.

Douglas A. Irwin, "How Clinton Botched the Seattle [WTO] Summit," *Wall Street Journal,* December 6, 1999, p. A34.

Jack L. Goldsmith & John C. Yoo, "Seattle and Sovereignty," *Wall Street Journal,* December 6, 1999, p. A35. The authors note with irony that the same groups opposed to the WTO for its lack of democratic controls favored the Kyoto convention imposing restrictions on countries as well as human rights treaties that would bypass Constitutional safeguards for American citizens.

Editorial, "Liberals and Social Order," *Wall Street Journal,* December 9, 1999, p. A26. "It was Mr. Clinton, several weeks before the [WTO] event, who said in the course of a very long news conference that he was glad the protesters were going to Seattle and that their grievances were legitimate."

Barun S. Mitra, "WTO Protesters vs. the Poor," *Wall Street Journal,* December 9, 1999, p. A26. "Then there was the young lady who looted a downtown shop while talking on her cellular phone…a desire to impose their own Luddite vision on the rest of the human race. Choice is anathema to these activists."

Charles Krauthammer, "President's Seattle [WTO] Stunt Completely in Character," *Seattle Times,* December 13, 1999, p. B4. Clinton derailed the WTO talks and gave aid and comfort to the street protesters.

Rachel Zimmerman, "Seattle and Its Mayor Face Fallout from Disturbances at WTO," *Wall Street Journal,* December 13, 1999, pp. A2, A10.

Scott Pelley, "The New Anarchists," CBS-TV, *60 Minutes II*, December 14, 1999. Interviews with the anarchists who smashed store windows in Seattle during the WTO meeting. Pelley did not ask who elected them saviors of the planet or their refusal to accept responsibility for property destruction by wearing masks.

Anon., "The Real Losers," *The Economist,* December 11, 1999, p. 15. "These five billion live in the developing countries, and include the poorest of the world's poor. They are the real losers from this whole sorry episode [of protest in Seattle]."

Anon., "A Global Disaster [at WTO meeting]," *The Economist,* December 11, 1999, pp.19–20.

Anon., "The Non-Governmental Order: Will NGOs Democratise, or Merely Disrupt, Global Government?" *The Economist,* December 11, 1999, pp. 20–21. Self-appointed special interests groups from Greenpeace to organized labor pose threats to legitimate governments.

Anon., "NGOs" Sins of the Secular Missionaries," *The Economist,* January 29, 2000, pp. 25–27. More often than not, NGOs are financed by governments!

Mike Carter & David Postman, "Unrest Even at the Top During [WTO] Riots," *Seattle Times,* December 16, 1999, pp. A1, A24. Disagreement by federal, state and local officials on how to deal with protesters.

Rob Eure, "Seattle is Again Besieged, This Time by ACLU, Other Post-WTO Suits," *Wall Street Journal,* January 26, 2000, pp. NW1, NW3. Eure writes "For Seattle, the World Trade Organization hangover is just beginning."

Michael M. Phillips, "A la Seattle, Activists Target Davos Economic Summit," *Wall Street Journal,* January 26, 2000, p, A17. Phillips writes "The social and environmental activists who helped sink last year's Seattle trade talks are now converging on the ultimate elite party: the World Economic Forum…in Davos, Switzerland."

Steve Stecklow, "How a U.S. Gadfly And a Green Activist Started a Food Fight," *Wall Street Journal,* November 30, 1999, pp. A1, A10. A profile of Jeremy Rifkin and Benedikt Haerlin. "Genetically modified food, Mr. Rifkin predicts, will become 'the single greatest failure in the history of capitalism in introducing a new technology into the marketplace.'" [This will occur only with the compliance of the media and the band-wagon of hysteria displayed over silicon breast implants, the Alar scare, nuclear power and tobacco!]

Peter Huber, "Ecological Eugenics," *Wall Street Journal,* December 20, 1999, p. A26. PH discusses suit against Monsanto on anti-trust grounds. They don't hope to win but led by Jeremy Rifkin, they seek a platform and publicity. Jeremy Rifkin "wants nobody in the genetic technology business at all." The ratio of land for food to land for people occupancy is 6 to 1, higher in poor countries. PH also reports that North

America now absorbs more carbon dioxide than it emits! And has more forested land than in 1920! [As Luddites they seek to stop gene research as well as its application. Or in essence "ecological eugenics" we abort this now!]

6

Game of Caricature

> Nixon was always the beneficiary of what, for want of a better term, might be called the Multiple Bad Things Advantage.
>
> —Herbert Block

By another name, human caricature is card stacking personified. On the editorial pages of the press across the land, for political cartoonists, there is a single illustrated frame available for comment and opinion. By contrast, cartoonists such as Doonesbury have several frames and a continuing narrative. But this is the exception.

For the most part, the effectiveness of political cartoonists is not unlike the thrust of ads. There is a need for a gimmick or metaphor to stop the reader from glancing elsewhere. If the metaphor contributes to the comment so much the better. But the stock in trade of all cartoonists is caricature, the visual equivalent of card stacking.

Usually some physical aspect of a person receives exaggerated prominence whether it is the face, nose, smile, etc. To be sure, some individuals more so than others lend themselves to caricature such as Boss Tweed, Joseph McCarthy, Lyndon Johnson, Charles De Gaulle, Nikita Khrushchev, Richard Nixon, Ronald Reagan and Bill Clinton.

For over thirty years from the 1940s through the 1970s, Richard Nixon had been the darling of political cartoonists, initially as a representative, then senator, then vice-president, then would-be governor, and finally president with the ignominy of resignation from that high office. From his early days, he received the appellation of "Tricky Dick." For cartoonists, Nixon was made to order with jowly jaws, five o'clock shadow, and a nose that invited extension.

At the same time that Nixon was establishing his fame and notoriety, the junior senator from Wisconsin, Joseph R. McCarthy emerged in February of 1950 as a fellow prowler after communists and subversives in our land. McCarthy had similar facial qualities that made him a favorite of cartoonists, none more so than Herblock of the *Washington Post*.

Nikita Khrushchev of the former Soviet Union was another favorite for cartoonists with his round face and rotund body making him a natural for satire.

For the cartoonists, persuasion is everything. Thus over simplification is the essence of the cartoonist's skill and handmaiden to the rhetoric of politicians who indulge in glittering generalities, card stacking, and other techniques enumerated above. Finally there is a symbiotic embrace, if not a love/hate syndrome, between politician and cartoonist.

Having skewered his victim, the caption is often unnecessary to the "message" of the cartoon, but if adroitly used, a one-line caption will reinforce the visual motif. Beginning with Thomas Nast, the power of cartoonists to shape public opinion has been clear. With the exception of Nast who, besides skewering Boss Tweed of Tammany Hall, also chose as his victims the Barons of Wall Street, most cartoonists confine their arts to the political arena or to some current issue.

Free Time Activities

IDENTIFY cartoons in your daily papers and news magazines as to the following:

1 what is the gimmick or metaphor?
2 is there caricature present?
of what? of whom? for or against?
3 propaganda techniques?
4 layout of the cartoon:
  a clear?
  b cluttered?
5 is the meaning clear?

AN EXPERIMENT:

1 xerox cartoons from newspapers or magazines;
2 then colorize the cartoons with crayons or ink; then
3 compare the black and white cartoon to the colorized one.
4 what effect(s) does color have on the cartoon?
5 which cartoon do you take more seriously?
6 why?

Game of Caricature Note

Herbert Block, *Herblock Special Report* (New York: W.W. Norton & Co.,1974), p. 9. On page 83, Herblock writes "During much of his career, I had pictured the Nixon face with 'five o'clock shadow'…Sen. Joseph McCarthy had one too. But I wouldn't have pictured it if had not seemed to me to fit what I considered to be their political thuggery."

Syd Hoff, *Editorial and Political Cartooning* (New York Stravon Educational Press, 1976). Over 700 cartoons are illustrated in this fine compendium.

Bill Mauldin, *Up Front* (New York: Henry Holt & Co., 1945). A collection of Mauldin's World War Two cartoons.

Francis X. Clines, "Caricature in the Age of Political Correctness," *New York Times*, March 30, 1997, Section 4, p. 3. "The heirs of Daumier are going too far as fast as they possibly can." The article also mentions the covers of the *New Republic* and *National Review* lampooning the high and mighty.

7

Game of Wit

Since brevity is the soul of wit, And tediousness the limbs, and outward flourishes, I will be brief.
—Shakespeare, *Hamlet,* Act II

As the political cartoonist reduces complex issues to a parody of a place, symbol or individual in a single frame, so the aphorist reduces complex social issues to a simple principle. In short, both cartoonists and devotees of wit are engaged in card stacking, and the "tight shot" discussed below in the media game.

The dictionary defines aphorism as a noun: a terse formulation of a truth or sentiment; a concise statement of a principle; a short, pithy, and instructive saying or formulation. Whether we call them aphorisms, epigrams, or proverbs, they are the product of mental agility and acute observations of people, places and things. This mental glitter is a game of wit.

These mini-concepts could have made their appearance in the game of errors, however their power and brevity deserve an extended play.

>>*On behavior*:

1) Murphy's Law: if anything can go wrong, it will.

2) Chisholm's Second Law of Human Interaction: any time things appear to be going well, you have overlooked something.

3) Finagle's Law of Sad Sacks: once a job is fouled up, anything done to improve it makes it worse.
4) Rudin's Law of Decision Making: in a crisis, people choose the worst option.
5) Salinger's Law of Success: quit when you're still behind.
6) Santayana's Law: a fanatic is a person who having lost sight of his purpose redoubles his efforts (stridencies, bomb throwing, demonstrating for the sake of demonstrating, etc.).
7) Ruby's Principle: the probability of meeting someone you know increases when you are with someone you don't want to be seen with.
>>*On communicating*:
1) Carr's Law: the role of reason is inversely related to the size of the crowd.
2) Wicker's Corollary: the greater the distance from the source, the more likely that lies and distortions become truth.
3) Law 444: the puffery of rhetoric is in direct proportion to the distance from power or office.
4) Gummidge's Law: the amount of expertise varies inversely to the number of statements understood by the general public.
5) Hirschman's Principle of the Hiding Hand: *selective* ignorance in the face of great challenges elicits great efforts.
6) Venus Syndrome: total ignorance ushers in the perfect society.
7) Weiler's Law of Effort: nothing is impossible for the man who doesn't have to do it himself.
8) Law 606: good intentions are inversely related to competence.
9) Law 369: beliefs are inversely related to what exists.
10) Matz's Maxim: a conclusion is the place where you got tired of thinking.
11) Thomas' Law of Reality: if men define situations as real, they are then real in their consequences.
12) Hobson's Choice: this one, or nothing.
13) Gresham's Law: the inferior (e.g., money, ideas, emotions, etc.) drives out the superior item or good.

14) McLuhan's Iron Law: the medium is the message.
15) Occam's Razor: nix on trivia (also known as the law of parsimony).
>>>*On politics*:
1) O'Brien's Law: the more campaigning, the better.
2) Legum's Law of Opposites: a candidate always says the opposite of what he means and predicts the opposite of what he thinks would occur.
3) Rakove's Law: the citizen is influenced by principle in direct proportion to his distance from the political situation.
4) Perkin's Law: in a two party system, people vote against the party they most want to defeat.
5) Dicey's Dictum: legislators prefer old maps for new territories.
6) Law 700: government in triplicate insures mediocrity, but does not deter corruption.
>>*On pedagogues*:
1) Shaw's Dictum: those who can, do, those who cannot, teach.
2) Law K12: teacher dedication is inversely related to remuneration.
On institutions:
1) Parkinson's Law: work expands to fill the time available for its completion.
2) Wicker's Law: government expands to absorb revenue and then some.
3) Peter Principle: in any organization, every person is promoted to his level of incompetence.
4) Shanahan's Law on Committees: the length of a meeting rises with the square of the number of people present.
5) Law 707: the edifice complex ratifies institutional apogee or decline.
6) Olney's Law: with time, the interests of public regulators and institutions merge.
>>*Odds & ends*:
1) Ettore's Observation: the other line moves faster.
2) Kauffman's First Law of Airports: the distance to the gate is inversely proportional to the time available to catch your flight.

*

What follows is a concept that does not fit easily into the aphorism mold but since it sheds light on human behavior it too deserves extended quote. The concept could just as easily have been placed elsewhere in this work. From Isaiah Berlin's well known seminal work, we have:

>>*Concept*: *hedgehog vs. the fox*: "the fox knows many things, but the hedgehog knows one big thing."

Definitions: the person who lives the life of a metaphorical *hedgehog* finds a mental haven in systems, wholes, or a central motif or organizing idea that provides an explanation for much of life—"a single, universal, organizing principle in terms of which alone all that they are and say has significance." Bacon would have recognized these potential recruits in universal systems as practitioners in the idols of the theater.

As to the behavior of the *fox*, this person pursues countless varieties (whether consistent or contradictory) of impulses, ideas, and ends. If there is a center, it is less logical than psychological. These persons "lead lives, perform acts, and entertain ideas that are centrifugal rather than centripetal, their thought is scattered or diffused, moving on many levels, seizing upon the essence of a vast variety of experiences and objects for what they are in themselves, without, consciously or unconsciously, seeking to fit them into, or exclude them from, any one unchanging, all embracing, sometimes self-contradictory and incomplete, at times fanatical, unitary inner vision."

>>Examples: "Dante belongs to the first category, Shakespeare to the second; Plato, Lucretius, Pascal, Hegel, Dostoevsky, Nietzche, Ibsen, Proust are in varying degrees, hedgehogs; Herodotus, Aristotle, Montaigne, Erasmus, Moliere, Goethe, Pushkin, Balzac, Joyce are foxes...Tolstoy was by nature a fox, but believed in being a hedgehog..."

>>Comment: the terms may be applied to individuals to illustrate certain predispositions of temper and mind. Moreover the description "can be made to yield a sense in which they mark one of the deepest dif-

ferences which divide writers and thinkers, and, it may be, *human beings in general*."

Berlin's conclusion deserves to be underlined since advertisers, politicians, cartoonists, lobbyists, and other practitioners of persuasion in the public realm run up against the wall of human temperament that acts as a brake against persuasion.

Free Time Activities

IDENTIFY by running down the list of witticisms, the corresponding concepts that they may illustrate from throughout this work.

IDENTIFY by making a two-column list of many public figures such as politicians, environmentalists, do-gooders, journalistic pundits and assorted "idealists" as to whether they are hedgehogs or foxes.

Game of Wit Notes

Anon., "[Irony] A Quiet Joke at Your Expense," *The Economist*, December 18, 1999, pp. 67–68. "Both irony and sarcasm involve saying the opposite of what you mean…Many people, when hearing an ironic remark, may not realize it is meant in jest."

Isaiah Berlin, *The Hedgehog and the Fox* (Mentor Books: New York, 1957), pp. 7–8, 11 (italics added).

Arthur Bloch, *Murphy's Law, Book Two* (Price/Stern/ Sloan: Los Angeles, 1980). Four items were taken from this work: Kauffman, Ettore, Matz and Ruby's Dictums.

William Safire, "Ploy," *New York Times Magazine*, January 9, 2000, pp. 20–21. On the uses of ploy, ruse, gambit, tactic and stratagem.

8

The Game of Doing Good

With mere good intentions, hell is proverbially paved.

—William James

Is doing good subject to persuasion? In this chapter we explore the contours of benevolence as well as review its various manifestations. In Chapter three we observed how modern advertising strives to keep consumers in a buying mood. In a narrow sense, a good consumer maximizes his satisfactions by harking to self-interest alone. Yet many consumers donate a portion of their incomes for charitable purposes. Of course these preferences and tastes do not exist in a vacuum. Contributing to the shaping of tastes are family upbringing, education, experience and of course modern advertising.

In chapter four we looked primarily at how politicians sought office. While social studies teachers have sought to inculcate civic imperatives, politicians have settled for the citizen's vote. Is being a good citizen subject to persuasion? Perhaps more so than the role of consumer concerned primarily with mundane matters. Whereas, the citizen is asked episodically to consider matters that involve matters of conflict, and still others of social neglect. From whence come these voices of civic concern? Before turning to the consumer and citizen, we take note that sandwiched between the proverbial good consumer and good citizen is the good Samaritan.

GOOD SAMARITAN

If we had to choose a word to describe altruistic behavior of this variety, we would select, spontaneity. The examples are common in recognition if not in number as when a person stops at the scene of an accident to render first aid; or when a person runs into a flaming building to rescue children, pets, or the infirm; or when individuals dive into a river to rescue the passengers of a downed airliner. When asked after the event, why they did what they did, the response is invariably, that it was the only thing to do. This is one of the most generous impulses of human behavior that counts not the cost. Spontaneous, generous, episodic and addressed to the particular circumstance are these good works. Needless to say, these good works are priceless and exceptions to ordinary behaviors. Nor can this benevolent impulse be captured, or reduced to a course of study and taught. Nor is this type of benevolence subject to persuasion.

GOOD CONSUMER

Obviously, we are all consumers dispensing our incomes in a manner that brings satisfaction to ourselves and our families. Advertising moves, as we noted above, on the premise that our appetites are to be catered to while the economist's model of rationality of consumer behavior assumes a finely calculating mind taking account of wishes, and pleasures but also noting factors that may cause us to postpone today's, in favor of tomorrow's, pleasure; or by abstaining from personal consumption, we may donate part of our income to education, medical research and community agencies.

As consumers we are more likely to contribute annually to an agency whose service is *understandable*, its discharge *necessary* and its cost *rea-*

sonable. These criteria are not unlike the prudent consumer's search for value in the marketplace.

Yet the consumer's quest for value in goods and services, for honesty in exchange, and for promptness in payment while serving self-interest also serves to stiffen the fabric of society. If the marketplace is open, competitive, and rewarding, then its contribution to the well being of its members is enormous and taken for granted. But like all institutions and mechanisms, it can be corrupted and destroyed in the name of a higher purpose. The marketplace is not the proper venue for spiritual solace, or as an avenue for affection. But the market does elicit the necessary supply to meet consumer demands. Thus Adam Smith's "invisible hand" of interacting self-interests serves the public weal. In other words, *perfect strangers* willingly do good for each other via exchanges in the marketplace.

GOOD CITIZEN

Looking back on our school days, we have differing memories of our social studies classes. Did we study our national history, our geography, and how a bill became a law amidst the study of "current" social problems? Since 1918, when the Kingsley Commission of the National Education Association issued its report on the cardinal principles of secondary education (with one of the seven planks on the duties of citizenship), the social studies teachers of the land have had the mission of preparing the young in their civic duties.

But what qualities are required of the good citizen in pursuit of the common weal? For one the citizen is called upon to balance self-interest with public spiritedness. Secondly to recognize the tricks and stratagems of persuasion, thirdly to avoid the common errors of thought, and lastly, to discharge the duties of citizenship while enjoying the benefits of civil life.

The duties are not onerous despite the flailings of teachers and the hovering shadow of Thomas Jefferson's crusade against ignorance. If students and citizens have taken their civic homework lightly, they nonetheless have paid their taxes, voted, and served, when summoned, on jury duty. They have also volunteered or have been drafted into the armed forces, and otherwise acted on the principle of live and let live.

Despite instruction, countless citizens have chosen not to do their civic homework of keeping informed. When politicians announce tax hikes, citizens retort that politicians are crooked and public employees are lazy. Nor, as we shall discuss in the following chapter, has the media helped citizens to be properly informed as to the pervasive role of government in our lives.

But there is a vital role for the good citizen that is often ignored in the above instruction. Nowhere are the limits of good citizenship, on the one hand, more likely to be probed than by the commission of crime, and on the other hand by the Not-in-My-Backyard (NIMBY) syndrome. Consider first the costs of crime. They can be accounted for by adding up the dollar expenditures for police, prosecutors, defense attorneys, courts, and prisons, and insurance premiums as well as the direct personal and property losses to the families of victims, to the police killed or maimed in the process and to society.

If crime is as ubiquitous as water, and if the criminal justice system continues to command a relatively high price for its services, then society must prudently reconsider the use of such expedients as better street illumination and the use of block and neighborhood surveillance by citizens. The streets can be retrieved for law-abiding individuals. Forsome critics these actions are seen as palliatives that bypass the "root causes" of crime. On the other hand, pleas for social justice as the ultimate cure for crime ignore the fact that crime is not a homogeneous activity.

Does poverty mostly cause crime? "The truth is just the opposite," William Tucker informs us as "*Crime causes poverty*". He goes on to say that "Poverty is the historical rule, the place where all societies began. The real question is how some societies ever overcame their original poverty. The answer is, through cooperation." And when cooperation is not at hand? Tucker replies that "Too much energy must be spent on self-protection, and too little time is left for the trust that can lead to beneficial enterprise."

Another example comes to mind in a different setting. Angelo Pellegrini in *Immigrants Return* speaks of peasants in southern Italy who in the past often harvested crops *before* they were mature to preclude neighborly theft of their crops. All suffered since the crops were picked early thereby diminishing the yield of the harvest and reinforcing the suspicion and lack of trust that thwarted "beneficial enterprise." Pellegrini noted, "When one began cutting, the rest followed suit."

Also common sense informs us that crime is not a homogeneous product like milk. Those engaged in shop-lifting often have credit cards and cash on them; also, white collar thefts on the job and white collar drug-users are examples of individuals who commit crime for motives other than poverty. The pursuit of the American Dream may lead some to short circuit the road to riches as Ivan Boesky and others on Wall Street have revealed. And long before drug money was splashed around, some politicians and law enforcement officials were susceptible to bribes.

A second social truth involves not only the magnitude of crime but also the disorder that diminishes freedom of action. Numerous families have understood without recourse to courses in sociology or economics, that peaceful homes and neighborhoods constitute a desirable public good.

What makes a peaceful neighborhood? Who will be the good citizen to practice restraint? Who will organize the neighbors? Who will call the police? Who will fight city hall? To deter marrings of the public peace requires forbearance. But to achieve such a common weal is often time consuming and costly for parents, clergy, teachers and employers in inculcating self-restraint in their charges. But the cost is even greater in a community out of control.

Let us consider the limits of good citizenship for a moment longer. Why is "*whistle-blowing*" by good citizens so rare a calling? Is the short supply of civic idealism a result of apathy, inferior education, or lack of models to emulate? If public officials are not too anxious to have their competence and honesty publicly questioned, and if criminals take a dim view of would-be witnesses, then what motivates the solitary individual to blow the whistle on defense program cost over-runs, political corruption, bribery, and other public wrong doing? Do such rare citizens calculate finely their personal risks against a much larger moral and civic imperative? Or do such individuals simply hearken to a different drummer?

As for the link between citizenship and controlling crime, the fact remains that individual prudence and civic duty are often at variance with social necessity, that what is good for the many may be detrimental on occasion to the solitary good citizen. At times, public virtue and private happiness may be at odds. Because even the good citizen's life is likely to be circumscribed by the three blunt realities of life: work, family and neighbors. Hence for many individuals, being a good citizen usually involves costs that exceed if any the intended personal benefits. Accordingly, society has great need for those individuals who throw caution to the wind, pursue civic virtue, regardless of cost, and repair the community's fabric.

As crime grows, the community's fabric remains frayed. Aside from attempts to corral crime, another approach has been to rehabilitate criminals. Each year government funds are sought for therapeutic programs in order to rehabilitate and reform drug addicts, alcoholics, drunk drivers, child molesters, rapists and other prison inmates.

Also, laws are passed banning cigarette smoking on airlines and in public places. For their own good, drivers are compelled to buckle up, and bike riders are compelled also to wear helmets. Aside from helmets, some motorists disobey speed limits; display cowboy behaviors on the road and by such behaviors invite accidents. Thus despite laws and therapeutic programs, errant social behaviors persist.

Even when doing good is self-imposed, for example, many attempts falter, for example, attempts to lose weight. Observing such behavioral barriers, Amitai Etzioni has concluded that human beings are not so easy to change. Thus doing good for others, much less for one self, does not flow as easily as water down hill. Is doing good a foolish exercise in futility? Much less subject to persuasion?

In this regard, with hindsight, we are no longer certain as were the architects of the The Great Society during the 1960s of the efficacy of the war on poverty: that dumping money on the "problem" would eliminate poverty and crime. Alice Rivlin, a budget official in the Johnson and Clinton Administrations, has noted that "Even the liberals are no longer sure they would know what to do if they had more to spend for social services, or *that it would do much good*."

Putting crime aside, the other pole of civil society concerns the slide from citizenship into crass consumerism. The NIMBY syndrome is alive and well across the land in opposition to the *erection and construction*, among others, of high rise apartments, prisons and jails, public housing, half-way houses, incinerators, factories, homeless shelters, sewer plants, and especially of airports. Public progress may come but only by beggaring-thy-neighbors with the fall-out of noise, congestion, dirt and other undesirable side effects. In short, the social compact according to NIMBY states that: "we'll take the benefits of these structures but better in someone else's front yard!"

Curiously its obverse exists in the opposition to the closing of military bases, veterans and community hospitals, schools, and fire stations that confirms the NIMBY syndrome of narrow consumerism. Thus the potential loss of jobs and services provides the rationale *to keep it in my backyard.*

Can these consumers be persuaded to step-up to their role of enlightened citizenship in pursuit of the common weal? By politicians? By the media? By the social studies teachers of the land?

Professional do Gooders

If the costs for the individual of pursuing civic virtue are costly, then surely professionals engaged in altruism are desirable? For example, Ralph Nader called our attention in the 1960s to the hazards of owning a Corvair car and transformed himself into an institution replete with acolytes in subsidiary movements around the country ready to tackle a myriad of public issues. But to whom is Nader accountable? What are the primary sources of his funding? His acolytes, for example, in Public Citizen took part in the WTO demonstrations in Seattle.

Still another organization, Common Cause was launched to maintain a weather eye on politicians and to keep the public interest above the clamor of private pressure groups. Their primary concern has been attempts at campaign reform, principally reducing the role of money in elections.

Beginning in the 1970s, a spate of organizations once confined to parochial matters was reborn as agencies of the public interest. With new social issues aborning every minute, these entrepreneurs of "altruism" found a fertile field of causes whether it was civil rights, abortion, capital punishment, disarmament, abused children, battered wives, gay rights, death row inmates, the homeless, nursing home deficiencies, the neglect of the handicapped, prison overcrowding, and various environmental topics. These social issues are real, but the questions remain: what can be done? For how long? At what cost? By whom? But most importantly, who *defines* these social issues?

Interestingly enough, a number of environmental groups have abandoned the Good Citizen model in a number of ways. First they have rejected an older role of collecting and disseminating information to its members and friends. Secondly after rejecting the rational model of persuasion, they have entered the political arena as skillful lobbyists. Legislators and their staff members are now buttonholed, campaign contributions donated, media reporters flattered and courted, and civil suits launched. The education of the public is now forsaken in favor of political power. Why? It is cheaper, quicker and easier to influence a relatively few legislators and judges than to "persuade" millions of citizens who might hold *contrary* views on environmental use.

These activist special interests masquerading as public interest groups are now lumped under the rubric of non-governmental organizations (NGOs). While springing from the civil society, these organizations, for the most part, have never looked back to the family, churches, schools and community agencies as the touchstone of a vibrant society. Their alarms are national and international in scope.

Acting under the banner of the saving the planet, these lobbyists of the Good Earth have offered *speculative diagnoses* of national and global disasters, *costly solutions* in terms of money and diminished freedom, and with a touch of *hubris*, that they are in possession of information that lesser mortals are denied.

As with other social issues, environmental matters of air and water pollution as well as the disposal of toxic and other wastes are issues in search of solutions. What is not clear today is whether regulation of the national EPA variety, or the alternative demands for zero population growth, or the freezing of technology at present levels, or the locking up of forests will "solve" these problems.

And if the supply of these national social issues appears unlimited guaranteeing life-time employment for the advocates of this or that cause, the solution to these advocates seems clear: more federal funds, regulations (and implicitly, higher taxes and, if necessary, budget deficits). But are all issues of equal merit; are federal and state funds unlimited, and what are the trade-offs to society of special interests working in the guise of the public interest?

In chapter three we noted the truism that poor nations have no need for advertising, nor do they have the means to impose environmental controls. Only rich societies can afford the luxury of both advertising and economic changes that reduce harmful discharges and truly cleanse the environment. The WTO protesters in Seattle ignored this elementary fact. But it made for "good" propaganda.

Consider air pollution and the automobile. Rather than give up the family car and turn to car-pooling and public transit, there are alternatives. One such alternative includes a car that burns natural gas that emits very few harmful gases. Such cars and trucks exist today. Tomorrow the electric car may prove feasible. These alternative solutions rely on individual self-interest rather than on Draconian edicts of "thou shalt not do..."

Yet edicts and regulations multiply. What continues to give impetus to these special interests is the willingness of the federal judiciary to grant these third parties *standing* in civil suits to sue and to receive attorneys' fees when victorious which in turn feeds the growth of further litigation. In short, the judiciary perceives these special interests as disinterested white knights donning the mantle of civic virtue. But do the sums of these disparate efforts equal the public interest? Moreover, are these particular interests at variance with each other? Finally are these self-proclaimed special interests at variance with business lobbies?

Not only have these special interests received legal standing to sue for the putative public interest, but they also have utilized the due process clause to great effect. While due process may be viewed as simply a procedural issue, the endless use of due process can nullify public and private actions. Court suits are costly in terms of time and money. Thus due process in willing hands becomes a tool akin to card stacking in the judicial realm.

Does society need these legions of alleged white knights because individual acts of public disinterestedness are rare and fraught at times with peril? Perhaps what has emerged is less a fastidiousness with the public interest, however defined, than a *narrowing* of doing good. It is a narrowing since political control of land, business, homes and people appears to be the goal under the facade of altruism. For some doomsday proponents of imminent global disasters, both the continuance of individual freedom and democratic government are seen as outmoded luxuries.

Still other do gooders hold a world view that society must have perfection *at once* otherwise imperfect agencies and institutions have no legitimacy, no authority over our lives. One death row lawyer has opposed capital punishment since he averred that the law in many rural parts of the South is imperfect. Hence until the day of perfection arrives, imperfection and ambiguity reigns. In this perspective the imperfections of criminal behavior are tolerated while the *victims* of crime are both neglected and denied the symbol and substance of justice.

Ironically Ellul notes that "Intellectuals are most easily reached by propaganda, particularly if it employs ambiguity." No doubt many academics, lawyers, and journalists believe they are better informed than the general populace and hence merit the leadership of various causes where "ambiguity" of evidence flourishes. Yet when it suits the proponents' purposes not ambiguity but "certainty of consequences" are asserted as when, for example, the clear cutting of timber, or the use of nuclear plants, or the use of pesticides in farming, etc., are cited as "clear" public evils. More often than not, the evidence is incomplete, and the conclusions, to say the least, are speculative.

"Once again," Ellul goes on to observe that "propaganda does not base itself on errors, but on exact facts. It even seems that the more informed the public or private opinion is (notice I say 'more' not 'better'), the more susceptible it is to propaganda." So much so that "The greater a person's knowledge of political and economic facts, the more sensitive and vulnerable is his judgment."

Yet for some impatient idealists, playing the political game is too slow a process to their taste. Doing good may be an innate human impulse but its execution runs against human resistance by individuals who do not wish to be reformed by others. Unfortunately doing good may commence as a noble purpose but when faced with the recalcitrance of human will and temperament as well as institutional inertia, the temptation to turn to disruption, coercion and eventually terror becomes compelling to the idealist. In this view, people must be liberated from their paltry lives. But such activists are not likely to heed Alfred North Whitehead's caution that "Ideals which are not backed by exact knowledge are mere fluffy emotion, and often lead to disastrous action."

So by degrees, idealists turn into extremists who slip into terrorism. This slippery slope of good intentions was observed by Lionel Trilling when he noted that "Some paradox in our nature leads us, once we have made our fellow men the objects of our enlightened interest, to go on to make them the objects of our pity, then of our wisdom, ultimately of our coercion."

Consider the following spectrum of persuasion, an extension of the one introduced in chapter three.

Holy Terror	*Sweet Reason*
"fire & damnation"	"truth will out"

<<____>>

At the far right end, we have sweet reason. This includes the "sweetness and light" of Matthew Arnold's gentlemanly discourse on culture that "seeks to do away with classes; to make the best that has been thought and known in the world current everywhere…not a having and a resting, but a growing and becoming, is the character of perfection as culture conceives it…"

It also includes that epitome of sweet reason in political discourse, the League of Women Voters. At election times, citizens are urged by the League to stay informed and to vote. To that end the League disseminates information and also serves as a clearinghouse of civic information. Like the League, the social studies teachers of the country also belonged at one time to this wing of reason and rationality in political affairs. All this before political correctness invaded the schools.

Granted that the League of Women is a rare and valuable institution, if it did not exist, we would have to invent such an organization. Despite universal education the role of *sweet reason* in human affairs appears to play an uneven role.

As to the *plague of holy terror* in the world it is very much with us as the daily news bulletins inform us. The bomb throwers with their preference for totalitarian regimes share a contempt for open societies and parliamentary majority rule. On the edges of society socially and often underground, they nurse their plots. They are the self-appointed minorities and operatives from Oklahoma City to Tel Aviv that speak for humanity with bombs and bullets.

A number of grim historical illustrations comes to mind: 1) the Gestapo and SS in Nazi Germany who tortured, and then banished their victims to Auschwitz, Belsen and other infamous death camps; 2) the KGB in the former Soviet Union who dealt with its dissident victims either in mental hospitals or by banishment to the various Gulags in Siberia; 3) and Prince Kropotkin who urged the use of terror at the turn of the century in which the power of the bomb supplanted the power of the word. And this "advice" persisted despite open processes of change in Western democracies. The descendants of Kropotkin since the 1960s have included the Irish Provos, the Palestinian Liberation

Front, the Baader-Meinhof Gang, the Red Brigades and the Red Faction who have killed many innocent people in the name of "liberation." Of late, Osam bin Laden has been the leader of terror and death at American Embassies abroad.

On a different plane, the use of visual terror in benign contexts may numb for a short period, but old behaviors apparently reassert themselves. Some examples of the uses of shock therapy to change soldiers' behavior include World War Two Army films detailing the horrors of Venereal Diseases (VD), presumably to the effect that soldiers were hence forth to practice lives of chastity.

Another example included the showing of mottled teeth to impressionable young people in the 1950s not to show them the horrors of unbrushed teeth, but to illustrate the horrors of drinking fluoridated water.

A more contemporary example by educators involves the bringing of a demolished car [particularly if two or more students perished in the crash] into a high school assembly auditorium. The means are visual terror, the message: stop driving and drinking. For a while, the wreck is sobering and numbing. Unfortunately, shock like anesthesia wears off.

But this is still another reminder that there are *limits* to changing behavior, permanently, even if such efforts are proffered in the name of doing good. And no matter how skillful the means or how numbed the senses, in short order, "normal" behaviors reassert themselves.

Free Time Activities

WATCH, OBSERVE AND LISTEN to TV and press coverage of professional do-gooders. Does television news and the press present opposing views to the do-gooders? Locally or nationally? Equal time?

NOTE if TV and press reporters ask demonstrators: how many groups they belong to? When they last demonstrated? What they do for a living? Are they asked what satisfactions they obtain from demonstrating other than appearing on the nightly news? Do reporters acknowledge that the demonstrators are familiar figures?

LOOK for the *100 % syndrome and the standard of perfection*: in letters to the editors, on talk shows on radio and TV, press conferences of parents with afflicted children seeking "government solutions", in political speeches and in the utterances of institutional do-gooders.

Doing Good Notes

Books

Robert N. Bellah et al., *Habits of the Heart* (Berkeley: University of California Press, 1985), especially chapter seven, "Getting Involved."

Willard Gaylin, Ira Glasser, Steven Marcus, & David Rothman, *Doing Good: The Limits of Benevolence* (New York: Pantheon Books, 1978). The Trilling quote appears on p. 72.

Mancur Olson, Jr., *The Logic of Collective Action* (New York: Schocken Books, 1968).

T.R. Reid, *Confucius Lives Next Door* (New York: Random House, 1999). The Confucian value system makes do-gooders redundant.

Alice M. Rivlin, *Systematic Thinking for Social Action* (Washington, D. C.: The Brookings Institution, 1971), p.69.

William Tucker, *Vigilante: The Backlash Against Crime in America* (New York: Stein & Day, 1985), pp.182–183.

Periodicals

Anon., "The Non-Governmental Order: Will NGOs Democratise, or Merely Disrupt, Global Government?" *The Economist,* December 11, 1999, pp. 20–21. Self-appointed special interests groups from Greenpeace to organized labor may pose threats to legitimate governments.

James Bovard, "Jubilee Time at Farmers Home Admini- stration," *Wall Street Journal*, April 26, 1988, p. 30, where Bovard notes that "Farm credit handouts are a classic case of ill-conceived humanitarianism. The more the government helps each individual farmer plant, the less all other farmers will receive for their harvest. Every time congressmen say they are helping a farmer, they are subsidizing all other farmers' competition."

Larry Brown, "Voluntary Time: Weekend Hours are Fine for Lending a Hand to Others," *Seattle Times*, March 19, 1988, p. C1.

Peter Collier & David Horowitz, "Slouching Towards Berkeley: Socialism in One City," *The Public Interest*, No. 94, (Winter 1989), 47–68.

Helen Dudar, The Price of Blowing the Whistle," *New York Times Magazine*, October 30, 1977, p. 41ff.

Amitai Etzioni, "Human Beings are Not Very Easy to Change," *Saturday Review*, June 3, 1972, pp. 45–47.

Rich Jaroslovsky, "Blowing the Whistle Begins a Nightmare for Lawyer Joe Rose," *Wall Street Journal*, November 9, 1977, pp. 1,35.

Paul Johnson, "The Heartless Lovers of Humankind," *Wall Street Journal*, January 5, 1987, p. 14.

N. R. Kleinfield, "The Whistle Blowers' Morning After," *New York Times*, November 9,1986, III, pp. 1, 10, 11.

Irving Kristol, "Symbolic Politics and Liberal Reform," *Wall Street Journal*, December 15, 1972, p. 8.

Irving Kristol, "New York is a State of Mind," *Wall Street Journal*, December 10, 1975, p. 20.

Lucette Lagnado, "For Those Fighting Biotech Crops, Santa Came Early This Year," *Wall Street Journal*, December 14, 1999, pp. A1, A8. An extensive network of NGOs funded by small foundations and networking rapidly. [Reinforces *The Economist* article cited above. They are self-appointed, and unelected shadow government with too little media scrutiny.]

Joann S. Lublin, "Disclosing Misdeeds of Corporations Can Backfire on Tattlers," *Wall Street Journal*, May 21, 1976, pp. 1, 11.

George Melloan, "What to Do When Your Own Lobby is Against You," *Wall Street Journal*, February 16, 1988, p. 33.

George Melloan, "Learning Political Science at Crop Genetics," *Wall Street Journal*, May 10, 1988, p. 35 is a short primer on the difficult process of introducing crop genetics to the marketplace. Melloan notes that "The truly remarkable thing is that one man named Jeremy Rifkin, neither a scientist nor representative of any established environmental movement, often has been able to stop such projects in their tracks."

Eric Morgenthaler, "Black Entrepreneurs Face Huge Hurdles in Places Like Miami," *Wall Street Journal*, May 17, 1988, pp. 1, 18. Morgenthaler delineates well the lack of "beneficial enterprise" when he notes that "William Calhoun has been in business in Liberty City for 15 years. During that time, his King the Tailor shop has been cleaned out three times by burglars and burned out once in a race riot."

Ted Pankowski, "United Way, Yes! But It's Not the Only Way of Giving," *Seattle Times*, February 19, 1988, p. A7.

George C. Smith, "Lawyers Split the Fee and Taxpayers Foot the Bill," *Wall Street Journal*, February 25, 1986, p.28. As Smith notes that "Even when the case is settled by mutual consent long before trial—and that is very common in cases involving busing, prison reform and employment discrimination—the plaintiff's attorneys invariably collect in full, just as though they had won in court. It's as close to a sure thing as there is in this uncertain world."

Jane & Michael Stern, "Decent Exposure," *The New Yorker*, March 19, 1990, p. 76. As one free-lance activist stated at a pro-nudist demonstration, "*Today, we protested all morning with the pro-choice people…Last week we were at the Oak Hill Country Club with the Anti-Apartheid Coalition. Next, we're going to a march with the gay community…*" (italics added).

Amy Stevens, "What Can a Lawyer Learn in One Day in Downtown L.A.?" *Wall Street Journal*, May 1, 1991, pp. A1,A9. The California Bar Association has instituted a one-day seminar in lieu of discipline for professional infractions.

David G. Stout, "The Lawyers on Death Row," *New York Times Magazine*, February 14, 1988, p. 46ff.

Elizabeth M. Whelan, "Apple Dangers Are Just So Much Applesauce," *Wall Street Journal*, March 14, 1989, p. A20, on the Alar scare.

9

The Media Game

> Were it left to me to decide whether we should have a government without newspapers, or newspapers without a government, I should not hesitate a moment to prefer the latter.
>
> —Thomas Jefferson, *Writings*, VI

Despite Jefferson's preference, in the modern world we require both a government and a press. Yet, in his time Jefferson viewed public ignorance as a grave threat to domestic tranquility. Public ignorance in his view would ill serve the people as a check on what politicians do or not do in the name of the common weal.

While the scope and impact of government on our lives has expanded enormously, the press coverage of government has not kept pace. Instead of vigilant and repeated investigations of the impact of taxes, programs, regulations and the dispensing of favors and privileges to industries and groups, the press has chosen to concentrate on the mechanics of elections and the personalities of politicians. In short the process is king, the end products of government ignored. Thus, Jefferson no doubt would be disappointed today at the press' predilection for chaff instead of substance.

To gain a foothold on what the press produces, consider what Henry David Thoreau had to say on the relationship of the reader to the press and the news. "Hardly a man takes a half-hour's nap after dinner, but when he wakes he holds up his head and asks, 'What's the news?' as if the rest of mankind had stood his sentinels...If we read of one man robbed, or murdered or killed by accident, or one house burned, or vessel wrecked...we never need read of another. *One is enough.* If you are acquainted with the principle, what do you care for a myriad instances and applications?"

Not much has changed since Thoreau's time despite the advent of the telegraph, telephone, radio, television, satellite transmission, satellite phones, fax machines and the Internet. Despite the innovations in communications, the content of the news media remains the same. Fires, earthquakes, tornadoes, floods, hurricanes, drought, murders, drug wars, assassinations, freeway pile-ups, political campaigns and war. News junkies and disaster buffs have never had it so good.

"Sock it to sock it to me sock it to me . . !"

If Thoreau returned for a visit today, he would not be surprised at the gimmickry and the hype of the press.

What do the media, (newspapers, news magazines, radio and television news) produce? Shielded by the protection of the first amendment, the role of the press in a free society has been to provide news. Traditionally the press has informed, entertained, and sought to persuade. But the latter is not limited to the editorial pages. Nor are television news reporters chastised for palming off opinions and speculations as news without the obligatory "commentary" tag at the bottom of the screen. If the press and television news are engaged in fact in persuasion then the media game must be added to the preceding ones covered in this work.

Engaged as the press and broadcast news are in *card stacking, disaster mongering, transfer, bait and switch, and equivalence* among other techniques then the question is how often are they in the persuasion business? Before that question is broached, consider the logistics of the press.

Most daily newspapers have 45 to 55 per cent of their pages devoted to commercial and personal want ads. The rest of the pages is left to features, comics, the weather, love-lorn columnists, food pages, social page, the sports pages, and finally to the less than 10 per cent for the news and commentaries. Like other businesses, newspaper are conscious of the demographics of their readers and market accordingly. Thus, various sections of the paper are separated so different members of the family or friends can read what they like and when. To imitate television, color once restricted to headlines has been splashed on as the example of USA Today attests. In short, the press has received its facelift.

On the other hand, television network news currently allocates out of thirty minutes, twenty-two minutes to news with eight devoted to ads. Normally the anchor or the reader of the news pauses and intones, "and now these commercial messages." We may not be far away from the day when the commercials will leave off with an announcement "and now back to these brief news messages."

What is the difference between selecting the news and rigging the news to suit a given bias? Daily, editors and reporters are engaged in selecting from the *potentially* infinite numbers of events, those that are fit to be printed or broadcasted. While the number may be infinite, editors are constrained daily by space and time limitations. Secondly, the nation's editors usually exclude overseas events unless they are disasters. As always disasters have precedence. In a manner of speaking, the disasters print themselves and fill the airwaves with pictures.

More prosaically, the wire services (Associated Press, United Press International and Reuters) daily feed their stories to print and broadcast editors who again decide what stories to use or what parts to supplement with their own reporter's accounts. Next editors must decide what stories to lead with, what space or time to allocate to each, or what stories to delay without going stale—all of these are professional decisions without overt political bias.

Whether on the front or back pages, story selection and rigging may arrive at the same layout of the news, one unwittingly, the other wittingly. Nor do selection and layout come out of a blank slate. In fact like everyone else, editors have a wallpaper of the mind patterned by experiences, education, thoughts, ambitions, feelings and goals to draw upon.

Aside from the play of disaster news and the limits of time and space, consider the press' obsession with spot news and scoops. Typically, to find information about jobs, homes, investments, appliances, cars, and travel destinations requires time, effort and money. As one foreshortens the time in which to obtain it—"I need it today!"—the cost rises sharply. To obtain vital information within 24 hours is more expensive (overtime and other costs) than allowing a week or a month for its orderly acquisition.

If "relevance" is of the moment, then the economic price for this instant news service is sky-high. Why is this? Because the price for media services (like health care) is paid for largely by third parties: advertisers largely for the media's' output and (employers and insurance agencies for health care). The newsstand price for newspapers would hardly cover the capital costs much less the costs of labor, overhead and supplies.

Thus removed by degrees from the disciplines of a free marketplace where consumers determine the quantity of a given item they are willing to purchase at a given price, the press and television news offer paradoxically not what time can permit but what time finds costly, and *very perishable.*

For the most part, the obsession with scoops is irrelevant in an electronics/computer/satellite/cell phone/Internet world of information because of its excessive cost and inaccuracy. Where does this obsession lead? For one thing, *jumping to conclusions.* We have the familiar rush to judgment whether in covering war time battles, airplane crashes, racial incidents or the return of a soldier from the Persian Gulf only to be shot on his doorstep—the latter reported as an implicit indictment that America is not a safe land. But *a week later*, the story took a new twist. It was not a random killing, but as it turned out one for hire.

How ephemeral is the news? For example, the early edition of the morning run is soon replaced by a later one, the paper serving finally as a garbage can liner while TV news vanishes like fireflies into the night. In short, the press' production of spot news serves as so much time and space *filler*. In this setting, spot news may be unique, and costly but hardly recyclable as well as an imperfect and clouded mirror to reality. For the reader and viewer, this spot news serves as junk food of the mind.

Aside from the press' present mindedness, there is the favorite use of the dramatic *reductionist technique* when reporting both disasters and non-disasters alike. As Nicholas Von Hoffman has written of television news that "the tight shot is actually our preferred way of presenting stories, people and events. The tight shot is just as prevalent in print journalism." In short, any significant issue that affects society whether it be war, nuclear plants, pollution, the homeless, etc., can be "reduced" to one "typical" critic, poor family, taxi-driver, worker, victim, etc. Then by sleight of voice-over, the reporter or anchor implies that the "one" covers thousands or millions of people in similar plight or conviction! Yet if public pollsters reported their findings of public opinion based on a sample of "one", the howl from the media would encircle the globe.

So when the media gives us the benefit of their findings based on one example, we have implications run loose, or jumping to conclusions. There are many examples. If one nuclear plant has trouble, then all nuclear plants are suspect; if one racial incident occurs regardless of context, it proves that the society is racist to the core; if one corporation dumps toxic chemicals into a river, then all corporations are suspect. At this juncture, given the tight shot or reductionist mode, the *media are unwitting practitioners of jumping to conclusions, card stacking and the trick of equivalence.*

What other side effect does the reductionist mode of news produce? Von Hoffman adds, "we are less interested in truth than we are in reality." Instead of issues such as the conditions of war and peace, of economic growth, of crime and drugs, and the dead weight of taxes and government regulations, we are given instead *doses of reality* not the complex truth. We get the "warts and all" of reality of mikes thrust into the unsuspecting faces of bereaved relatives at scenes of disaster. But as Von Hoffman adds, "neither a wart nor anything else can make sense without a background, a matrix, a context." Another writer, David Marquand, cited above, has made a similar point about the need for "philosophic musing" to give details a context.

If not, we face the conclusion that the *news has no meaning.* We are inundated with a pile of jigsaw-puzzle pieces that do not make a picture.

Another uncomfortable conclusion to be drawn is that the media prefers to arouse feelings, to foster social cleavages and, to spark fires rather than to shed light.

Another aspect of the "tight shot" is the artificial little world created. Let me explain. We watch as the camera pans to the faces of the angry demonstrators who are shouting obscenities, waving placards, finger gesturing and taunting the police, etc. But the TV cameraman does not zoom back, nor does the print reporter broaden her gaze, to show the street or the neighborhood. Is this "demonstration," in fact, a minor blip in the community? An *exception*?

But as seen on the nightly news, this demonstration gives the impression as if the entire city is in thrall. More clearly, what might we see if another camera across the street zoomed-in when the TV cameras left? Very likely, the demonstrators turning-off their TV performances? This street theater is the very heart of reality presentation but not part of understanding an issue within a context. Oddly enough the media remains an unwitting accomplice to this manipulation, this card stacking by activists who cultivate and exploit the media's penchant, especially the need of television news for dramatic stories that are confrontational. The WTO meeting in Seattle is only the most recent example.

Equally interestingly, the networks and press have become addicted to superficial coverage of the federal government but not to its costly and pervasive penetrations throughout our economy and society. Instead TV reporters stand before the White House, or on the Capitol steps, to *speculate* on what might have happened and what *might* occur. Volumes of glittering generalities pour from the trench coated reporters. We have the tight shot of *one* voice, par excellence. While some reporters are assigned to specific beats such as the Pentagon and the State Department, the concentration of coverage is on the President and occasionally a congressman or senator. Or until some scandal or other "natural" story breaks. Meanwhile, neither the intrusions of government bureaucrats into our lives, nor the power of committee chairmen in Congress receive the sunlight of exposure. Nor the lack of oversight by Congress of what it has spawned.

Rather than substance and meaning, the expedient arithmetic of covering *one* president or a *few* senators [rather than 100 senators, 435 congressmen and their burgeoning staff as well as a thousand federal judges] prevails. Instead the networks and the press welcome the *filler* of the Presidential campaign *two years before the election* with its endless primaries, countless interviews, endless predictions and polls—in short the trivia of process. What is a weary citizen to do as endless testimonials of movie stars, plain folks and athletes all urge him to join the bandwagon to the White House? Zap the so-called news, read a book or perform a community service?

It is as if the networks and the press preferred to cover the "spring training" of baseball rather than the season of substance. Yet days after this or that primary or caucus what understanding does the public gain of its political machinery? This saturation coverage would give a visitor from another country the impression that all normal life has come to a halt in breathless anticipation of primary results.

Again, Von Hoffman is apt when he observes: "Have you noted how much political writing deals with the humdrum mechanics of conducting a campaign?" He concludes that where the tight shot, the lack of context and trivialization prevail, the result is that "speech is converted from communication to formula." To the media this "formula" is welcome news.

Another by-product of this card stacking is that politicians and the media *mutually define* the issues to be reported. In so doing, they both choose what *not* to discuss. In short, the press and politicians *mutually agree* to remain silent on the heavy hand of government subsidies, programs, regulations, and taxes. The Sunday television programs, for example, provide politicians at the national level with free airtime to sell their government "solutions" unencumbered by other guests or speakers offering alternative solutions from the marketplace or from the voluntary non-profit sector of society. In turn, the questions popped to politicians are soft ones, and the politicians reciprocate with glittering generalities and a call for an endless expansion of government programs and bureaucracy. To most politicians, the media serves as a domesticated and self-serving megaphone, Watergate aside. Reporters are rarely critical of the role of the press in not covering the performance of government from the federal level to the school district. "The only way a newspaper can effectively monitor the government is to get access to computer tapes," asserts Elliot G. Jaspin, a Pulitzer Prize-winning reporter.

Only the public suffers from this myopia by the media. For example, the polls invariably reflect displeasure with how government is not working on the federal and state levels. Even when presidential candidates are elected reflecting the polls, the symbiotic embrace between the media and politicians thwarts the will of the people. Only when the Congress attempts a quick hike in pay is the wrath of the public immediately manifest. Otherwise, the cost over-runs, the duplications and corruption of many government programs roll on. Then the media is surprised when the savings and loan scandal explodes onto the front pages and the nightly news. Nor are we told of the penchant of government programs to produce unintended negative social consequences that just happen and multiply. Are not good intentions sufficient?

Another story that just seemed to happen concerned the explosive growth of state government employees throughout the 1980s. While New York State's population, for example, grew by 2 per cent, its state employees grew by 30 per cent. In the same period, while New York City's population remained flat, there was a 25 per cent increase in city employees. Since the media failed to cover this story, the citizens of the state were at a distinct disadvantage.

Returning to the tight shot, we would add to the tactic of grand omissions, the parallel twin of compression. The latter distorts the scale of events and renders a different aspect of reality. The easiest way to illustrate this notion is by watching a movie in a theater and then viewing the same film on videotape. For some movies it does not matter, but with "Lawrence of Arabia" and "Dr. Zhivago", it does. Nor is it a matter of truncating lush backgrounds and scenery, important as that may be, but rather the *alteration of scale* from 70mm wide screen to 27" video screen that leads to dissimilar and distorting experiences to the viewer.

Similarly "facts" and "events" from one medium turn into "propaganda" in another medium. Compression and distortion takes place because of *"translation effects"* of messages from print to television to print and back to television. For example, an incident may be reported as follows. A press reporter may cover the issue in 300 words; a radio report reduces it to 15 words; a television account runs to 40 words and 30 seconds of film; and finally a news magazine uses one small photo and 50 words.

By dealing with exceptions as routine news rather than a full exploration of a social issue in the context of historical background, time, groups, and numbers involved, the press slides into the persuasion business with *card stacking* its primary thrust and modus operandi. Caveats are in order. This is not a plea for "good" news such as bake sales, Boy Scout meetings, church socials, etc. Nor is this a plea for a three-ring circus. Walter Lippmann observed in the 1920s that the American people could only stand one big circus at a time. Since most individuals are rooted in work and home affairs, the outer world and its events must take their turn like other distractions. Finally the reports by the press that earn welcome Pulitzers remain exceptions rather than the rule.

Typical news items are, by definition, not news. From the press' dismal coverage of the economy comes an obvious example. Monthly the press and TV news tells us of the unemployment rate for the nation, but not the employment rate, that is, the percentage of the population working. Instead the metaphor that best captures the tilt of press and television coverage of the economy is that the "glass" of the economy is *five per cent empty* but not the extraordinary other fact of *ninety-five per cent* abundance.

Even if the metaphorical glass were 99.9 per cent full, the media would stress the 0.1 per cent emptiness. Of course, unemployment and pockets of poverty exist in our society. But despite these imperfections the testimony of millions who long to come to our shores appears to escape the notice of editors and reporters. The result is an extreme form of card stacking.

Another preference for exceptions occurs daily in the reporting of crime, of criminals and the horror of the death penalty, but rarely of the victims of crimes, or of the spill-overs onto families, and to the disorder of the community. Why are criminals such favorites of the press? As presumed underdogs, criminals are exceptions, again.

Of the media's Vietnam coverage of 1968, Peter Braestrup observed in *Big Story* that "Television's show-business tradition put little premium on breadth of coverage, fact-finding, or context. Brave as he often was, the television journalist in Vietnam was preoccupied with film and logistics, with little incentives to seek out sources or investigate nonfilmable aspects of events." Braestrup has touched on the heresy of television news, if it's not on film the event did not take place. If no photos exist, then the events slide down the Orwellian black hole of forgetfulness.

In February of 1968, the North Vietnamese launched the Tet offensive. For the media there was an instant rush to judgment that the North Vietnamese had won and that the US had lost the battle, and implicitly the war. It was not true, but for six weeks and well into March 1968, that was the line repeated ad nauseam by print and broadcast reporters. Peter Braestrup noted of the media's coverage of the war that "In overall terms, the performance by the major American television and print news organizations during February and March 1968 constitutes an extreme case...Rarely has contemporary crisis-journalism turned out, in retro-spect, to have veered so widely from reality."

Braestrup concluded that this media exercise in persuasion was an "extreme case."

Aside from the war, 1968 was a traumatic time for many Americans. Across the land from San Francisco State to Columbia University, college campuses were strewn with student protests. Were the so-called students protesting the draft, the Vietnam War, civil rights or their alleged desire to govern the institutions? But the press did little to reveal the background, motives, funding and goals of the non-students and sundry groups protesting on campuses and streets.

The press' lack of contextual coverage came to a head during the 1968 Democratic Party Convention in Chicago and the associated street riots. As noted, perhaps, someday, an historian or two will give us an objective review of what happened in 1968, but television will merely dust off its video morgue every ten years or so with new voice-overs so that the "reality of 1968" remains undisturbed. Ironically, Peter Braestrup concluded that lop-sided coverage of the Tet Offensive could be repeated by the media. In fact, only six months later, the media, especially television in the summer of 1968, repeated the misinformation by card stacking of the political convention and street games by "peace activists."

But of course the coverage of the Tet Offensive, and the Democratic Party Convention in 1968 were not exceptions as to how the media worked day in, day out. Even public views in poll findings revealed distrust of the media and implicitly of media malpractice.

More recently we have witnessed card stacking and exceptionalism on daily view from the first day of Desert Shield in August of 1990 to Desert Storm in January of 1991. At first with no pictures and reports from the Kuwaiti victims of invasion, the networks filled up their airtime with endless *speculation* by armchair politicians, retired military men and so-called peace activists. Meanwhile the print media filled its spaces with maps, tables and pictographs of the relative sizes of the military hardware.

Secondly, war protesters received *twice* as much air and print coverage as supporters of President Bush even when the polls were two to one in favor of the President's actions in the Persian Gulf. Again peace protesters from A to Z received prime time coverage even though they were a small minority in the larger society. The reductionist mode again.

Who can be against peace among nations, and domestic tranquility within nations? But simply wishing for peace and a crime free society does not banish the reality of evil in individual and group behaviors. Or for that matter, governments willing to use force for national self-interest. Shouting, screaming, marching and demonstrating are psychological safety valves but they do not change certain unpleasant facts about human nature and a plethora of conflicts from the individual to the global level.

Returning to the Persian Gulf War, the media continued to report as *fact* after January 16, 1991, that war had begun on that day instead of August 2, 1990. So, now the war "glass" was half empty.

Did Cable News Network executives insist that if Iraq permitted one reporter in Baghdad, that CNN should be permitted to have another one in Kuwait City? Of course Saddam Hussein would have nixed that deal. So CNN settled for telling us the *one-sided* horrors of US bombing of Baghdad but not of the systematic rape and pillage of the Kuwaiti people that began on August 2, 1990. Nor of the destruction and despoliation of the environment by Iraqis blowing up oil wells and pouring oil into the Persian Gulf. With the war over, Kuwait received even less coverage after the first few days. It was old news and time to move on to other stories. So the cameras turned to the disaster enveloping the fleeing Kurds. And then to Somali, Haiti and on to Bosnia and Kosovo.

True to form in both the Vietnam and Persian Gulf War, the media did very little in terms of background other than provide splendid maps and the weather, but failed to report on the history of the nation and region, its people, religion, and their way of life. Instead they remained far away just exotic people and places.

Closer to home we had the specter in 1996 of black church arson fires. From the President on down to black spokesman, the assumption was that racial hatred was the cause of these fires. The media at first heaped gasoline on this volatile mixture. Gradually, the media recovered its senses and reported the facts. Michael Kelly's long article in *The New Yorker* reviewing the media's coverage is a public service.

Finally the prognosis by the media for better coverage and contextual reporting may be sidetracked by a number of factors. With time scarce, as noted, ersatz substitutes flood the market with "reality' leading the parade. *Affluence too may be the ultimate enemy of meaning.*

If so the human preference to be amused will be served. Thus understanding, problem solving and truth seeking must take a back seat. Realists in the media will cite this barrier: they will improve their product only when the public demands a better quality one, or when public education improves, or when…Thus the proponents of the status quo in the media find solace in this human threshold.

What are the implications of a media devoted to the pursuit of trivia? For one, it makes the world safe for advertisers, politicians, media pundits, political cartoonists, and special interest groups, especially dogooders. For another it permits these individuals and groups to co-opt, if not manipulate and use the media, for its own purposes that may be at variance with the public interest, broadly construed.

In the meantime, the media game drones on. While we have truth in lending disclosures, we await the equivalent of truth in reporting from the media.

Free Time Activities

ATTEND, if *time* permits, demonstrations and press conferences of politicians and "professional" protesters. Then observe the press and TV coverage of the same. Note besides the editing, *what is left out*, what remains? Do you agree that minor matters were dropped but that the substance is conveyed accurately?

VIEW the World BBC-TV News and for those close to the Canadian border the Canadian CBC-TV network's nightly news round-up may prove instructive in receiving different perspectives on the news. Or do the BBC and CBC ape the American TV networks in style and lack of substance?

READ your local newspapers to see if statistics are used as parts of stories on public issues. Are the statistics perfunctory and add little or nothing to the story? Are they in number form only or are pie-charts, bar graphs, and pictographs used? Are there civic topics not covered? Are there monthly updates on local, state and government programs as to effectiveness and costs? Is there a monthly digest of government statistics on the cost of government department by department, program by program?

READ, for those with foreign language skills, the foreign press especially for stories on topics such as trade and tariffs, foreign policy, military alliances, etc. How does the foreign press compare to our domestic coverage of the same topics?

Media Game Notes

Books

Peter Braestrup, *Big Story*, Anchor Books (Garden City, N.Y.: Anchor Press/Doubleday, 1978), pp. 508, 523–524.

Edward Jay Epstein, *News From Nowhere* (New York: Vintage Books, 1974).

Jack Fuller, *News Values* (Chicago: U. of Chicago Press, 1996). Fuller acknowledges that the primary function of the media ought to be the review of government performance.

Marshall McLuhan, *Understanding Media* (New York: McGraw-Hill, 1965).

Henry David Thoreau, *Walden*, (New York: Modern Library, 1937), pp. 84–85.

Periodicals

Anon., "We Woz Wrong," *The Economist,* December 18, 1999, pp. 47–48. A rare display of a publication recounting the errors it made during the year.

Josh Barbanel, "Why Did New York (City) Hire 49,000 Worker in Seven Years?" *New York Times*, Sect. 4, October 7, 1990, p. 5. Paul Duke, Jr., "Boomtown Budgets Suddenly Are Pinched as Tax Takes Dwindle,"

Wall Street Journal, April 3, 1991, pp. A1, A6. For state-by-state data, see *Wall Street Journal*, April 17, 1991, p. A16.

Ken Colston, "Newspaper Forsake Their Strength: Words," *Seattle Times*, January 31, 1988, p. A15.

Henry Fairlie, "An Englishman Goes to a Klan Meeting," *New York Times Magazine*, May 23, 1965, p. 26ff. Fairlie attended a KKK meeting which included an attempt to burn a cross. But he concluded, "How the camera can lie! There was nothing as melodramatic or as eerie in this ritual as the color photographs, carefully trimmed for effect, suggest…But the old rugged cross would not burn," p.84.

Michael Gartner, "Local Newspapers Ignore Their Own Main Streets," *Wall Street Journal*, February 2, 1989, p. A15.

Robert Goldberg, "Broadcast News, Soviet-Style," *Wall Street Journal*, June 6, 1988, p.17. Speaking of the US and USSR television coverage of the Reagan/Gorbachev summit in June of 1988, Goldberg observed "both manage to miss the big picture. For different reasons—the US focus on viewer appeal and the USSR focus on the party line—both Soviet and American viewers came away with only partial glimpses of one of the most over reported stories of our era."

Robert D. Hershey, Jr., "Hearings on Capitol Hill and Who They Attract," *New York Times*, (National Edition) May 6, 1988, p.11.

Peter W. Huber, "Manufacturing the Audi Scare," *Wall Street Journal*, December 18, 1989, p. A10.

Peter Huber, "The Death of Old Media," *Wall Street Journal*, January 11, 2000, p. A26. The merger of AOL and Time Warner signals an important shift in the media. To whose benefit?

Alex S. Jones, "Rethinking Newspapers," *New York Times*, January 6, 1991, Section 3, pp. 1,6.

Monica Langley, "Campaign Camera Crews Angle for Best Shot, Which May or May Not Be a Candidate's Best Side," *Wall Street Journal*, May 25, 1988, p. 52. Langley notes, "It is often the camera operator's *artistic* pictures, more than substance, that determines what's shown on TV news," (italics added). Another example where the lens of the camera provides a distortion not only of "reality" but also of context.

Dave Marash, "There's More to Local News Than Fender-Benders," *New York Times*, July 2, 1989, Sect. 2, pp.25, 30.

Patrick M . Reilly, "Knight-Ridder Makes A Costly Effort to Engage its Readers," *Wall Street Journal*, December 6, 1990, pp. A1, A9.

David Shribman, "TV's Election Coverage Busily Skims the Surface While Bemoaning Candidates' Lack of Substance," *Wall St. Journal*, April 11, 1988, p.48.

Smith, Helen Matthews, "AIDS: Civil Liberties vs. Lives," *Wall Street Journal*, September 13, 1994, p. A16.

Smith, Helen Matthews, "The Deadly Politics of AIDS," *Wall Street Journal*, October 25, 1995, p. A18.

Stricharchuk, Gregory, "Computer Records Become Powerful Tool For Investigative Reporters," *Wall Street Journal*, February 3, 1988, p. 25. The

Elliot G. Jaspin quote appears in this article, but the press has been selective in using computer tapes to enlighten the public.

Nicholas Von Hoffman, "Capturing the Warts and All," *Seattle Post-Intelligencer*, March 26, 1976, p. A9.

Frank Wetzel, "Why Don't Newspapers Ever Have Enough Space?" *Seattle Times*, February 7,1988, p. A19.

Frank Wetzel, "A Graphic Exchange Between Ombudsman & Designer," *Seattle Times*, January 31, 1988, p. A15. Wetzel, the *Times*' ombudsman engaged in a public debate with the *Times*' front page designer who found extraordinary qualities in photos "to impose order on chaos…to convey information faster and make it easier to find. They also impose a hierarchy on content."

Appendix A: Crime at 11 on TV News

Max Frankel, "Live at 11: Death," *New York Times Magazine*, June 15, 1997, p. 20. Local TV stations present a never-ending diet of crime, catastrophes and other assorted disasters such as fires, etc. MF draws on surveys that people trust the TV anchors or reporters a good deal, more so than newspapers. [What we see, we trust, apparently. If it is not on TV or in the papers, to many people it did not occur! Do we have once more that proverbial tree that made no noise if no one was present? But then again how do we "know" it fell?]

Max Frankel, "Where There's Fear, There's News," *New York Times Magazine*, June 29, 1997, p. 22. More reporters than ever lament that there is no "good news" meaning wars, disasters, etc. MF recommends: "why not dramatize the known *causes* of cancer?" Then he cites Jerome Bruner about telling stories and the need of how to swim in a "sea of stories." MF sees a need of "how to construct stories, classify stories, check out stories, see through stories and use stories to find out how things work..." He insists that this should be the principal task of education. "Journalists, like teachers, are society's narrators." Neal Gabler would agree, too.

Max Frankel, "The Murder Broadcasting System," *New York Times Magazine*, December 17, 1995, pp. 46,48.

Max Frankel, "More on TV Mayhem," *New York Times Magazine,* January 28, 1996, p. 23. A follow up of his previous article stating that murder and mayhem are the principal diet of local TV. Many letters poured in agreeing with Frankel. One writer states that the constant showing of murder and mayhem leads to the perception that crime is everywhere when it is not. We have the tight shot, again. [Editors like politicians like to tell the "inside story" *after* they leave office, like St. Augustine on denial, but not quite yet!]

Ray Bradbury, "The Affluence of Despair," *Wall Street Journal*, April 3, 1998, p. W11. Hard hitting on the mindless repetition of the media especially the late night news with its steady diet of murder and mayhem.

Thom Gunn, "Isn't There More to Life Than [Reporting] Mayhem and Body Counts?" *Seattle Times*, September 2, 1997, p. B5. A look at the Times' August 14, 1997, pp. 1,2, with the results of local page 1: "The score four dead one maimed, one wounded. But the Times is just warming up." "Page 2's score: four dead, including one child...two maimed, and one baby shook up." "The final score for Local News is 24 dead (including six children and one dog), four maimings and two injured."

Lawrie Mifflin, "Crime Falls, But Not on TV," *New York Times*, July 6, 1997, Section 4, p. 4. The widening gulf between the drop in crime rates and what appears especially on local TV news. LM quotes Joseph Angotti, former VP at NBC News, who insisted that crime coverage is cheap: "It's the easiest, cheapest, laziest news to cover, because all they do is listen to the police radio, react to it, send out a mobile camera unit, spend an hour or two covering it and put it on the air."

Michael Winerip, "Looking for an 11 O'clock Fix," *New York Times Magazine*, January 11, 1998, p. 30ff. A look at Channel 2 in Orlando, FL, which switched from the usual crime lead in stories to others involving education, etc. and then watched their ratings plummet. In polls people say they want serious news, but at home they prefer to be entertained with disasters, crime, etc. [At 11 why would anyone want a serious look at anything?] MW is a staff writer for the NYTM.

ABC-Television, *American Agenda*, "Media Literacy," January 9, 1996.

Appendix B: Black church fires

Peter Applebome, "A Tragedy Is Transformed into a 'Miracle' in Mississippi Town: Racially Motivated Attack on Black Church Brings Smithdale Residents Together," *New York Times,* January 3, 1994, p. A6.

Ronald Smothers, "US Inquiry into Fires at Black Churches," *New York Times,* January 20, 1996, p. 6.

Eric Harrison, "Torching of Black Churches Stirs Civil Right-Era Pain," *Los Angeles Times,* January 20, 1996, p. A1.

Sue Anne Pressley, "Church Fires Rekindle Pain, Specter of Racism Rises With the Smoke," *Washington Post,* January 23, 1996, p. A1.

Kevin Sack, "Burnings of Dozens of Black Churches Across the South Are Investigated," *New York Times,* May 21, 1996, p. A6.

Eric Schmitt, "Few Links in Church Fires; Official Sees Racism But No Sign of Conspiracy in Firebombings," *New York Times,* May 22, 1996, pp. A11, A14.

Bob Herbert, "A Church Destroyed by Hate, Burned Down in Wave of Arson Directed at African American Churches in South," *New York Times,* May 24, 1996, p. A13.

Editorial, "An Epidemic of Terror: Wave of Arson Attacks Against African-American Churches in the South," *New York Times,* May 24, 1996, p. A12.

Anon., "Fire Destroys a Black Church in Alabama," *New York Times,* June 4, 1996, p. A12.

Anon., "Arson Strikes Black Church, 30th in 18 Months," *New York Times,* June 8, 1996, p. 6.

Ronald Smothers, "Church Sues Extremist Group Over Fire," *New York Times,* June 8, 1996, p. 6.

A. M. Rosenthal, "Color Them White; America's Blazing Churches," *New York Times,* June 11, 1996, p. A25.

Alison Mitchell, "Clinton, Citing Church Arson, Denounces 'Forces of Hatred'," *New York Times,* June 11, 1996, p. A11.

Stephen Labaton, "Suspects Are Held in Fires at 2 Black Churches in South," *New York Times,* June 11, 1996, p. A11.

Ronald Smothers, "2 More Black Churches Burn, This Time in Rural Mississippi," *New York Times,* June 19, 1996, p. A19.

David Gonzalez, "Joining Hands to Rebuild Church Ruins: Fund to Rebuild Burned African American Churches Started by the New York Board of Rabbis," *New York Times,* June 19, 1996, p. A19.

Todd S. Purdum, "President and Governors Confer on Fires—to Discuss Burnings of Black Churches," *New York Times,* June 20, 1996, p. A9.

Robyn Meredith, "Mixed Opinions About Role of Racial Hatred in Burning of Black Churches," *New York Times,* June 23, 1996, p. 10.

Ronald Smothers, "Same Liquid used in 2 Fires at Black Churches," *New York Times,* June 25, 1996, p. A9.

Anon., "Arson Suspected at Another Black Church," *New York Times,* July 1, 1996, p. A10.

Frank Bruni, "O'Connor Reaches Out After Fires: John Cardinal O'Connor Denounces Burning of African American Churches and Racism," *New York Times,* July 1, 1996, p. B3.

Anon., "Church Fire in Northwest: Arson Suspected at African American Church in Graham, Washington," *New York Times,* July 8, 1996, p. B7.

Anon., "Insurance Industry to Offer Aid to Black Churches Hit by Arson," *New York Times,* July 13, 1996, p. 9.

Robert A. Rosenblatt & Robert L. Jackson, "Girl, 13, Arrested as Probe of Church Fires is Pressed," *Los Angeles Times,* June 11, 1996, p. A1.

William Booth, "In Church Fires, a Pattern But No Conspiracy," *Washington Post,* June 19, 1996, p. A1.

Pierre Thomas & Michael A. Fletcher, "Arrests in Black Church Fires Racially Mixed," *Washington Post,* September 14, 1996, p. A10.

Michael Kelly, "Playing With Fire: Burning of Black Churches," *The New Yorker,* July 15, 1996, pp. 28–35. An acute analysis of the media's failure in reporting this story accurately.

Larry B. Stammer, "Recent Church Fires Run Against Trend; Safety: Insurance Records Show a Sharp Decrease in Such Blazes from 1980 to 1994," *Los Angeles Times,* June 22, 1996, p. A4.

Fred Bayles, Little Backs Racism Theory: Arsons on the Rise at Both Black, White Churches," *Seattle Times,* July 5, 1996, pp. A1, A2. Over an 18-month period ending July 1996, there were fires at 73 black churches and at 74 white churches.

Monica Langley, "Black Church Arsons Win Donor Millions—Now, How to Spend It?" *Wall Street Journal,* August 9, 1996, pp. A1, A4.

Joan Brown Campbell, "Racism and the Burning of Churches," *Wall Street Journal,* June 25, 1997, p. A23.

Bibliographic Notes

Although a number of the books cited contain somewhat dated references and examples, the exposition of themes for the most part remains as pertinent as ever in the works of Ellul, Hayakawa and Huff.

The question of what constitutes thought and knowledge has long antecedents in philosophy, religion and more recently psychology. Both the Dewey and Sowell books address themselves to this perennial issue.

As opposed to the games of persuasion, I would recommend Boorstin and Boulding's works which explore various *modes of thought* from an historian and economist's perspective. Applying rigorous methods and tools to current social issues, the works of Rivlin, and Wildavsky deserve close reading.

As to thought and persuasion, one of the best primers on the subject is Brown's work not only because it is well written but also because of the depth of information brought to bear on several subordinate themes including so-called brain washing.

The study of the meaning of words, the subject of semantics, was a then-current topic during the 1940s and 1950s. Hayakawa's work was a popular one in the field. Following the lead of the semanticists, there were adherents who believed that most human and institutional conflicts were due to ruptures of communications. Hence if we clarified our words, conflicts would either diminish or disappear.

As we noted above, the media has been remiss in presenting statistics often and in modern graphic forms. Nor has the media shown how numbers offer a "context" to the "tight shot." Of course, beyond numbers and percentages lie the intricacies of correlation and regression coefficients which the media studiously avoid. Clearly, Huff's delightful primer on statistics badly needs updating.

De Grazia's work is an historical exploration of time, while Linder's analysis of time requires close reading that will yield dividends of understanding. Finally McLuhan's aphorisms are welcome but "messages" after all need contexts. Otherwise avalanches of current events numb human consciousness.

Berlin, Isaiah. *The Hedgehog and the Fox.* New York: Mentor Books, 1957.

Boorstin, Daniel J. *The Image.* Colophon Books. New York: Harper & Row. 1964.

Boulding, Kenneth. *The Image.* Ann Arbor Paperback. Ann Arbor: University of Michigan Press, 1961.

Boulding, Kenneth. *The Meaning of the Twentieth Century.* Colophon Books. New York: Harper & Row. 1965.

Brown, J. A. C. *Techniques of Persuasion.* Baltimore: Penguin Books, 1963.

de Grazia, Sebastian. *Of Time, Work and Leisure.* Anchor Book. Garden City: Doubleday & Co.,1964.

Dewey, John. *How We Think.* Gateway Edition. Chicago: Henry Regnery Co., 1971.

Epstein, Edward Jay. *News From Nowhere.* Vintage Books. New York: Random House,1974.

Hayakawa, S.I. *Language in Thought and Action.* New York: Harcourt, Brace & Co., 1949.

Huff, Darrell. *How to Lie With Statistics.* New York: W. W. Norton Co., 1954.

Kuhn, Thomas S. *The Structure of Scientific Revolutions.* Chicago: University of Chicago Press,1970.

Linder, Staffan B. *The Harried Leisure Class.* New York: Columbia University Press,1970.

McLuhan, Marshall. *Understanding Media.* McGraw-Hill Papeback. New York: McGraw-Hill, 1965.

Rivlin, Alice M. *Systematic Thinking for Social Action.* Washington, D.C.: The Brookings Institution, 1971.

Sowell, Thomas. *Knowledge and Decisions.* New York: Basic Books, Inc., 1980.

Wildavasky, Aaron. *Searching for Safety.* Transaction Books. New Brunswick: Rutgers University Press, 1988.

About the Author

Currently, the author is a writer and an occasional arbitrator of consumer disputes for the Better Business Bureau.

Formerly, he has taught history and economics on the high school level; additionally for six years he taught adult education classes. On occasion he taught in-service professional classes to teachers. Also, he has served as an occasional instructor in the School of Education at the University of Washington.

For a decade as hearing examiner, he conducted student disciplinary hearings for the Seattle Public Schools. For three years he also chaired hearings of parental appeals of mandatory student busing assignments.

As to formal education, the author received his bachelor's degree from Queens College; and both his master's degree in economics as well as his doctorate in the history of education from the University of Washington.

Finally Garland published in 1996 his historical study, *The Schools in the Great Depression.*

Printed in the United States
6179